WHATEVER HAPPENED TO SHELL'S
NEW PHILOSOPHY OF MANAGEMENT?

Whatever Happened to Shell's New Philosophy of Management?

Lessons for the 1980s from a Major Socio-Technical
Intervention of the 1960s

F. H. M. BLACKLER
C. A. BROWN

Department of Behaviour in Organisations
University of Lancaster

with comments by

Michael Foster
Paul Hill

SAXON HOUSE

British Library Cataloguing in Publication Data

Blackler, F H M
    Whatever happened to Shell's new philosophy of
management?
    1. Industrial relations - Great Britain - History
    - 20th century
    2. Shell UK Limited
    I. Title   II. Brown, Colin Anthony
    658.31'5   HD8391

Published by
Teakfield Limited,
Westmead, Farnborough, Hants., England

Printed by Itchen Printers Limited, Southampton

ISBN   0 566 00306 6

Contents

Acknowledgements

The preparation of this book would not have been possible but for the generous help of the people in Shell
who so kindly gave us their time and help when we
researched the Company's programme to introduce a new
philosophy of management. To them we extend our thanks.
We would specifically like to mention Geoffrey Hibbert,
Miles Edge, Dan Rawlinson and Ken Fuggle who themselves
spent much time talking to us and who arranged for us
to speak to other people at Shell's Head Office and at
the Company's Stanlow, Shell Haven and Teesport
Refineries.

As the reader of this book will discover the research
findings we report here and our interpretation of them
are controversial. The organisation change programme
that is the subject of this book generated strong
feelings, both for and against, in the minds of many
people affected by it. Accordingly, the fact that it
is our judgement that the balance of research evidence
supports criticisms of the change programme may not be
agreeable to some people. Our particular thanks, however, are due to two people who do not agree with all
we say! Paul Hill was in large part responsible for
introducing the philosophy programme when he was
employed in Shell in the mid 1960's, and in 1971 Gower
Press published his book 'Towards a New Philosophy of
Management' based on his experiences with the exercise.
He has kindly allowed us to quote freely from his book
and at our invitation has prepared a record of his own
observations on our research that we are pleased to
publish in this volume. Michael Foster from the
Tavistock Institute of Human Relations was, as one of
the social science advisers to Shell, involved in
aspects of the change programme. We heartily thank him
both for his invaluable help during the conduct of our
research and also for allowing us to publish a letter
he wrote to us in which he states his reservations
concerning some of our conclusions.

Thanks are also due to the Social Science Research Council whose grants (nos. BE 707 and BE 710) provided the financial backing for the work we report here. Our typist, Miss Janet Fisher, deserves a special mention for the great care and patience she has shown in typing the book. We are most grateful for her efforts. Finally, we thank the following authors and publishers for permission to quote copyrighted material:

K. Kumar, Prophecy and Progress. Penguin Books, Harmondsworth, 1978.

R. May, Power and Innocence. New York, Norton, 1972.

J.R. Ravetz, Scientific Knowledge and its Social Problems. Oxford University Press, London, 1971.

M. Rein, Social Science and Public Policy. Penguin Books, Harmondsworth, 1976.

T. Roszak, The Making of a Counter Culture. Faber and Faber, London, 1970.

Frank Blackler
Colin Brown
Department of Behaviour in Organisations
University of Lancaster
Lancaster
England

PART I

INTEREST GROUPS AND PATTERNS OF INVOLVEMENT

1 Introduction

There is, as the maxim tells us, nothing so dead as yesterday's news. It is understandable, of course, that the concerns of the moment and the hopes of tomorrow are more likely to command attention than is any reflection upon yesterday's failures. Yet learning theory tells us that there is much to be gained from just such a reflection and that, despite its often depressing initial effect, analyses of cases where actions did not lead to their intended outcomes are indispensable for progress in the conduct of human affairs.

It is with these thoughts in mind that in this book we present the case of a major social science intervention of the 1960's and analyse the reasons for, and significance of, the developments that have been associated with it. In some respects, as must be any major attempt to change the way a company is managed the story we report here is a unique one. Yet we have come to think that it would be a mistake to think that the fundamental shortcomings we have identified in this case were, and remain, peculiar to it alone. The conclusion we have reached in our analysis of this case is that its more fundamental shortcomings are alive and well and may be found at the bedrock of many applied social scientific endeavours of the present day.

This is, however, to anticipate somewhat. The details of the case that we will describe begin in 1965 when a special study group in Shell UK Refining Ltd. that had been working for twelve months previously presented to the Company's top management its proposals on how industrial relations problems in the organisation might be overcome. Its suggestion was that a 'philosophy of management' should be specified and disseminated throughout the Company. Within this philosophy, it was proposed, recent behavioural science

3

ideas of good management practices should be incorporated.

The proposals were accepted and, after eminent social
scientists from The Tavistock Institute of Human
Relations had helped write the philosophy statement,
through 1966 and 1967 a series of conferences were held
in Shell Refining Ltd., widely involving staff in
discussion of the newly formulated series of
principles. Later, to implement the philosophy
demonstration job redesign projects were launched in
the Company, responsibility for implementing changes
implied by the philosophy was placed on departmental
managers, in a new spirit of collaboration with union
officials new terms and conditions were formulated for
weekly paid staff, and some of the philosophy's
principles were intendedly incorporated in a refinery
designed and built at Teesport around this period.
Thus through this project an effort was made first,
to articulate the assumptions upon which Shell managers
were to begin to manage their affairs then second, to
translate this into action which (in the light of the
philosophy) now emerged as appropriate.

As we discuss later, the project was of particular
interest to certain social scientists of the day and
has subsequently continued to attract their comment
and acclaim. Yet a reasonably complete account of
this story has never previously been published. It
was originally reported by a person intimately
associated with the launching of the project, Paul
Hill, in his 1971 book 'Towards a New Philosophy of
Management'. This account includes a postscript
written by Shell's major social scientific consultant
in the early days of the exercise, Eric Trist. Aspects
of the work were described also by Burden (1975) and
Taylor (1972). Without fear of contradiction, however,
it can be said that these are all somewhat 'rosy'
descriptions of what took place. Hill and Trist, it
is true, do include certain caveats (see Hill,
pp.183-9) but these are not the main subject of either
writers' analysis. Indeed Hill says at one point:

'Whether, therefore, the values and concepts of
the philosophy statement are now sufficiently
well embodied in the organisation to withstand
any future setbacks, it is still too early to
to judge. The indications are that they are,
but the next five years will show'. (p.186)

It is widely recognised now however, by social
scientists and others with more than a passing knowledge of the Shell philosophy story, that in these next
five years the project did not flower in the manner its
architects had hoped. Yet quite what did happen and
what lessons may be gleaned from the experience it is
harder to determine. Unfortunately the 1976 reprint
of Hill's book is of little help. Hill acknowledges
in the introduction to this edition the continuing
interest people show in the project and how useful a
resume of it would be. Yet believing that this would
require a great deal of research not then possible he
himself had not attempted such a review. Hill did,
however, comment that:

'In talking to people about the Shell
programme, one of the most frequent questions
they have asked was whether, in retrospect,
I felt that the approach adopted in 1965 had
been the correct one. My response has been
that, given the background history, the
circumstances at the time, the size of the
organisation and the complexity of the
problem it faced, the approach was certainly
appropriate and was probably the best that
could have been devised at that time. It was
also highly innovative. I still believe this
is true ....' (pp.xiii and xiv)

In the study we report in the following pages we
describe how, despite such enthusiasm on the part of
workers involved in the project, from very early on
the philosophy exercise achieved but moderate success.
There is no doubt about it we believe but that the
exercise failed, rather spectacularly, to introduce
a new philosophy of management to Shell.

5

One way to consider the story we record in the following pages is as a failed organisation change programme to study, in other words, the good and bad points associated with the particular organisation change strategy and tactics used in Shell in the mid 1960's. There are, certainly, a number of learning points that do emerge from such an approach. We are aware that there have been at least three attempts to change organisations through exactly the method first tried in Shell. One is mentioned briefly by Thorsrud and Emery (1976) as taking place in the Norwegian company of Norsk Hydro. A similar programme is documented rather more fully by Clark (1972) and took place in a company in Southern Wales. Both these programmes seemed to have been rather shortlived. Both also were certainly inspired by the same reasoning that led to Shell's programme, and were, in large parts, direct imitations of it. We do not know the genesis of the third case although its location certainly suggests similar links may exist. It is, we understand, currently (1979) underway at the Shell Sarnia Chemical Plant in Canada.

The study of the problems associated with a change strategy that appears to have a certain recurring appeal will be of interest, therefore, to students of planned social change. Indeed, read as a case study of a failed organisation development programme the story has an undoubted value and, as the words of the people who described the events will testify, a certain wry humour also. Yet, in tracing the course of events of the philosophy exercise in Shell we have become convinced that its significance is less to do with inappropriate change strategies used in it, important as the mistakes which were made undoubtedly are. Its more lasting significance lies, we believe, in the reasons why social scientists became involved in the exercise in the first place, the reasons why the Company accepted their advice, and the resulting functions that social science came to serve within Shell. The philosophy project in practice seems to have successfully re-established managements control of its employees at a somewhat difficult time for the

Company. Yet for most people involved it promised to
be doing rather more than this, seeking as it did to
set the scene for nothing less than a new role for
Shell in the community and purporting also to set in
motion a new relationship of partnership between
employer and employee. Why, in our view, the Shell
story may be of some general interest is that it
documents very vividly just how easily and substantially these fine ideals were, and may be, let
down. The whole episode amounts, we believe, to something of a cautionary tale for people who are, like us,
interested in improving society by the application of
certain social scientific notions.

At the time of our research into the Shell programme
however, we had no idea this would be our conclusion.
In 1977/78 when we did the work we were working on an
S.S.R.C. financed programme studying applications of
job redesign and in particular the reasons why
companies begin and subsequently develop or abandon job
redesign programmes. In this research we studied job
redesign in British Leyland where little or no work on
job redesign had been done, and in Volvo where, by
contrast, an extended programme had been in operation
for many years. This work we published in 1978. At
the time of this research however we were also
interested in examining a company that, unlike either
Leyland or Volvo, had begun job redesign projects but
later abandoned them.

Shell UK appeared just such a company, and in 1977
we approached managers at their Stanlow refinery in
Cheshire with a request to undertake a review of their
now long abandoned job redesign projects of the mid
1960's. Immediately we began the work, however, it
became clear that the job redesign experimentations
could not be studied in isolation from the rather more
extensive organisation change attempt of which it was
a part. We therefore switched our attention in this
case away from a narrow concern with job redesign alone
and began to study the broader progress of Shell's
new philosophy programme. To reconstruct this story
we spoke, often at considerable length, with a number

7

of managers in the company, union officials and some more junior level staff. We concentrated our efforts on the locations which had been the main target of the philosophy exercise. At Shell's Stanlow refinery we interviewed eighteen people about the main programme and six specifically about one particular aspect of it (the wax plant episode reported in chapter 5). At Shell's other main UK refinery, Shell Haven in Essex, we interviewed nine people. Also we spoke to two people at the Company's refinery at Teesport which was built around the time of the philosophy exercise, an ex-member of the central office team that had co-ordinated the whole philosophy programme, and a member of the Tavistock Institute of Human Relations who had been a member of the social science group advising the company. In addition we consulted published reports of the episode (Hill, 1971, Burden, 1975 and Taylor, 1972), a number of internal reports kindly made available to us, and an unpublished M.Sc. thesis (Hibbert, 1969) written on aspects of the programme by a member of the Shell head office co-ordinating group.

We should emphasise that we were not, in selecting the people that we should speak to, seeking to conduct an opinion survey on what people thought about the exercise. We did, certainly, learn a lot about what people do think but our main objective was to reconstruct the main sequence of the events that took place in the story. Thus, we spoke to people who we judged could provide information of this sort to us, later (as we report in chapter 7) checking out the accuracy of our reporting with a number of them before publishing this account. As we remark occasionally in the story, the accounts of our interviewees collectively reproduced a consistent pattern, so much so that we do now find ourselves confident about the general factual accuracy of the account we have been able to reconstruct.

We have prepared our account of this research in the following way. First (chapter 2) we describe the reasons why the Tavistock Institute of Human Relations became involved in Shell, what was of interest in the

request to write a company philosophy for the social
scientists at the Institute. Next (chapter 3) we
describe the published reasons why Shell adopted the
Tavistock inspired philosophy, the recollections of
people today about why the Company had become involved,
and finally compare these varying accounts as a prelude
to presenting our review of the exercise itself.

In the next three chapters the philosophy exercise
is reconstructed, as far as possible using the words
of people whom we interviewed. A number of conferences
were held to introduce Company employees to the ideas
in the philosophy. In chapter 4 we describe peoples'
recollections of these, setting these alongside Hill
and Trist's published descriptions of what had taken
place. Chapters 5 and 6 include the descriptions of
efforts next made to implement the philosophy, and
explanations of the processes by which these were, in
the most part, to come to grief.

In chapter 7 we summarise the themes of the previous
chapters and bring the story up to date by reviewing
the state of social science at Shell's refineries at
the time (1977/78) our research was underway. As the
reader will, at this stage of the book, be aware, our
research data is quite controversial, so damning is it
to the suggestion that the philosophy programme was a
success. In chapter 7 after reviewing the methodology
of our study, we are pleased to be able to include
written comments on our data by Paul Hill, who had
been closely involved in the original exercise and had
published the earlier account of it, and by Michael
Foster from the Tavistock Institute who had also been
involved in the programme. The last word, however, we
reserve for ourselves! In chapter 8 we analyse the
lessons that, in our view, might be learned from the
Shell story, reflecting back to the aims of social
scientists involved in Shell in the 1960's and forward
to the lessons it might suggest for the possible
endeavours of other social scientists in the 1980's.

2 Social Science

In the epilogue he wrote to Paul Hill's account of the philosophy exercise, Eric Trist identifies four phases of the involvement in Shell of the social scientists from the Tavistock Institute. These were the initial drafting of Shell's new company philosophy, the attempts to bring about value change within the Company in accordance with it, helping to work out strategies by which the philosophy could be implemented, and evaluating progress towards its implementation. Each of these phases presented its own interest and challenge to the Tavistock people and we consider them further in later chapters.

There remains, however, the prior question of how people from the Tavistock Institute regarded their general involvement; especially, was the exercise of particular significance to them? Trist's account leaves one in no doubt that it was.

Recalling Shell's request for assistance in working out a new management philosophy he mentions the two purposes he understood it was intended to serve – 'a guide to managerial decision making in a period of technical change', – 'a stabiliser during a period of increasing industrial unrest'. He recognises also certain constraints, in that the philosophy should be relevant to the Company as a manufacturing concern, be acceptable to management, unions and workers, and be related to establishing conditions favourable to productivity bargaining. Then, observing on the uniqueness of the Company's request to help formulate a suitable philosophy Trist states that the Tavistock:

> 'had one clue from some of our recent
> theoretical work as to why a company such as
> Shell might be in search of a new philosophy
> to manage its refineries. This work was
> concerned with identifying possible lines of

organisational response for enterprises confronted with the need to adapt to an accelerating rate of technological change under conditions of rising uncertainty and complexity (Emery and Trist, 1965). In this situation an organisation would only retain its cohesion and move in an appropriate direction <u>if the majority of its members subscribed to a common set of values</u>. These values would have to be relevant to the character of its tasks and to the emergent processes in its technology and environment. <u>The explication of a self consistent set of relevant values and the teasing out of their implications for all fields of the company's activities and for the needs of its employees at all levels would involve the formulation of a statement of philosophy</u>'. (p.96, emphasis added)

Reference to Emery and Trist (1965) gives more detail on the underlying ideas that Trist refers to here. The paper was entitled 'The causal texture of organisational environments' and is regarded as something of a classic in social science/management literature. In it the authors argue that a major organisational and social problem is that in the modern world organisations are increasingly becoming unable to control developments significant to their function and survival. Using the terminology of systems theory they argue that the environments in which organisations operate and exist are nowadays becoming dynamic, even turbulent to the extent that organisations may be unable to predict the effects of their own policies or to understand how the tide of significant events around them, which they have themselves helped to generate, may be ridden. The image presented is one of change, uncertainty, loss of control; an image indeed that catches preoccupations of the present day just as much as it awakened fears of managerial impotence and social collapse in the mid 1960's.

As this makes clear, the social scientists involved in the philosophy programme saw their work in the broadest of perspectives. Society, they believed, was in real danger of becoming unmanageable. For them, two related imperatives could be identified to deal with this threat. The first was:

> 'the emergence of values that have overriding significance for all members of the field. Social values are here regarded as coping mechanisms that make it possible to deal with persisting areas of relevant uncertainty. Unable to trace out the consequences of their actions as these are amplified and resonated through their extended social fields, men in all societies have sought rules, sometimes categorical, such as the ten commandments, to provide them with a guide and ready calculus'. (Emery and Trist, 1965, p.28, emphasis in original)

Second, is the related suggestion that organisations of many different types will need to co-operate more together, in a kind of coalition, recognising the legitimacy of each others existence. Certain consequences follow from this, namely:

> 'the determination of policy will necessitate not only a bias towards goals that are congruent with the organisations own character, but also a selection of goal paths that offer maximum convergence as regards the interests of other parties'. (op.cit., p.29)

The opportunity that the Shell project seemed to offer the Tavistock people did, therefore seem considerable. Part of the much larger Royal Dutch Shell group of companies it appeared to be in just such a turbulent environment as Emery and Trist's analysis suggested was likely to become more common. For example, there had been Suez and the beginnings of OPEC, this was an industry of high finance, of advanced technology, there was an emerging ecological lobby whose

12

activities promised to limit oil usage and to lead to
pressures on companies to pollute less, and there were
difficulties also in industrial relations in the
Company's refineries. To be able to help draft and
introduce a new philosophy outlining the company's
developing role in the modern world, and possible ways
of carrying out its emerging functions, must have
seemed a marvellous opportunity.

A further quotation from the 1965 Emery and Trist
paper confirms this latter point. Discussing their
vision of how organisations in the modern world should
form coalitions they note that this:

> 'implies what McGregor (1960) has called
> Theory Y. This in turn implies a new set of
> values. But values are psycho-social
> commodities that come into existence only
> rather slowly. Very little systematic work
> has yet been done on the establishment of
> new systems of values, or on the type of
> criteria that might be adduced to allow
> their effectiveness to be empirically tested
> .... Likert (1961) has suggested that, in
> the large corporation or government
> establishment, it may well take some ten to
> fifteen years before the new type of group
> values with which he is concerned could
> permeate the total organisation. For a new
> set to permeate a whole modern society the
> time required must be much longer - at least
> a generation, according to the common saying -
> and this, indeed, must be a minimum. One may
> ask if this is fast enough, given the rate at
> which (turbulent) environments are becoming
> salient. <u>A compelling task for social
> scientists is to direct more research onto these
> problems</u>'. (op.cit., p.31, emphasis added)

Theories and methodologies in applied social research
do not develop in a cultural vacuum. Whilst commentators may disagree as to the exact nature of the
relationship between any particular social and

organisational theory and the attendant culture, few would deny that a relationship does exist. The emergence, for example, of the core ideas of scientific management or human relations theory has been related quite closely to the social and political conditions of the time (see, for example, Friedman, 1955 or Braverman, 1974). In a similar fashion, of course, the concerns, values and approaches of the applied social scientists of the 1960's at the Tavistock Institute were related to the social and cultural concerns of those times.

Kumar (1978) has noted how the 1950's had 'marked something of a watershed' in the history of industrialism as a social system and as an ideology in its own right. Two points of view about the society of the day and trends for the future were, as he notes, emerging. The first of these was based on the apparent prospects for continuing economic growth, rapid technological development and the disappearance of class conflict. The famous comment by a British political leader of the time 'you've never had it so good' sums up the feelings of optimism characteristic of this point of view. Many social scientists became associated with this kind of position, citing apparent evidence of a convergence of eastern and western industrial societies and speculating about the possibilities for industrial development in the third world. Daniel Bell's 1961 book 'The End of Ideology' was, perhaps, the best known presentation of the 'embourgeousment' thesis that also impressed people at this time. Discussing the notions that underpinned these visions Kumar comments that they assumed:

> 'Developments were now once more on the right footing; further progress seemed assured; the main outlines of the future were already visible in the existing organisation of industrial societies'. (p.183)

In contrast with this analysis, yet paradoxically sharing something of the optimism of it, a rather different social analysis was beginning to emerge at this time. Kumar succinctly expresses this view as follows:

> 'There is the discovery, or rediscovery, of
> the dark side of industrialism. So far from
> having solved its problems, industrial
> civilisation seemed to have raised new ones
> in a form so acute that its very survival was
> at stake. The economic benefits of
> industrialism are seen to be purchased at the
> cost of increasing 'dis-economies' to the
> society at large: pollution, crowding, the
> exhaustion of the natural fossil fuels on
> which the industrial economy itself depends.
> The main currents of industrialisation –
> rationalisation and bureaucratisation – run
> into an impasse, and increasingly large-
> scale hierarchical organisation seem
> productive of inefficiency and irrationality'.
> (p.187)

Where, one might ask, is the optimism in this analysis? The optimism here, we suggest, was centred upon beliefs people held of the possibilities for achieving far reaching changes in social life and political order. The decade of the 1960's is rich with examples of hopeful attempts at such social changes, most notably in America with the development of flower power and other so called 'counter cultures' and in Europe with the May 1968 'revolution' in Paris. As we discuss further in chapter 8, characteristic of these and similar developments of this era is a confidence that change may be brought about by example, that once a new life style or form of organisation can be demonstrated as viable other adherents to the new ways would emerge. Indeed, just as embourgeousment and convergence theories were developed by social scientists adopting the more accepting social analysis so also were new ideas developed by social scientists favourably inclined to this more critical approach. The most obvious of these was T-groups and encounter groups, later to be embodied in programmes of 'organisational development'. Adherents of the T-group

15

movement, incidentally, often used a jargon that shared many of the phrases, e.g. being 'turned on' or 'tuned in' more normally recognised as associated with the youth drug culture of this time.

The analysis of social trends that Emery and Trist were developing in the early 1960's had strong links with the more critical, though still highly optimistic, social commentaries emerging at this time. In later years their analysis of turbulent environments was to be developed further by them into a world view suggesting that the loss of control and resulting uncertainty facing organisations in the modern world was indicative of the major upheaval facing us all as changes implied by new technologies transform society. New values, on this view, have to be accepted if the transition to new social forms may be achieved at all smoothly. Yet despite the fact dangers to this transition were acknowledged to exist Emery and Trist clearly believed (and believe still) that it can be achieved and that an era of unprecedented fulfillment will be the reward. For more recent statements of their views Trist's 1978 paper 'Technical, Economic, Social and Cultural Developments and their Implications for People in Organisations', Emery's 1976 book 'A Choice of Futures', or their joint 1972 book 'Towards a Social Ecology' may be consulted.

The latter book is of some interest to the Shell story. In this book reference is made to the Shell episode as a good example of what can be achieved by modern companies. In this book too may be found the clearest statement of Emery and Trist's analysis of conditions under which the transition to post industrialism may be facilitated. Organisational philosophies, they say, should be supportive of the emergence of new values. Organisation structures should become more flexible to reflect their complex environments. Inter-organisational relationships need to move from being predominantly competitive to being predominantly collaborative and a new negotiated order, based on a mutual accommodation of interests all of which are regarded as legitimate, should emerge.

Organisational objectives need also to be changed, with social, technical and ecological objectives being regarded as being as important as the more conventional economic objectives. Finally, organisations, according to Emery and Trist, should not regard the resources they handle as their own. Rather, resources, both material and human, should be regarded as belonging as much to 'society' as to the organisation itself.

At the time of the start of the Shell project in 1965 there were two other main strands in previous work by Tavistock researchers that were to be particularly relevant to the project. The first of these is 'socio-technical systems theory', the theory of job design for which the Institute is known world wide. In his description of relevant work done by the Institute interestingly enough Paul Hill concentrates exclusively upon this. Basically stated this approach argues that while technological considerations evidently imply constraints on the methods feasible in a given work situation so also do social and psychological ones. Early work by the Tavistock Institute (Trist et al., 1963) had illustrated this vividly in the British coal mines where the introduction of new methods of coal getting had disrupted previously well established behaviour patterns of the workers with unfortunate consequences both to productivity and to the workers well being. As evidence by the paper by Bucklow (1966) the promise of a new way of analysing jobs by focussing on both technological and social imperatives seemed highly promising and was to lead to the development of autonomous work group theory (Herbst, 1974), to much detailed work on the prerequisites of these (e.g. Gulowsen, 1972) and to the emergence of important social experiments in Norway relating job redesign theory to industrial democracy (see, for example, Thorsrud and Emery, 1976). At the start of the Shell project, however, all this was in the future. The socio-technical approach to job design was new and if it was to be adopted in Shell this would, in the minds of the Tavistock researchers, represent a major shift in managerial values of the kind they felt was so necessary for the modern world.

The second other relevant strand in previous work by
the Tavistock researchers that should be mentioned was
their work on resistance to changes or, as it was to
become known, on the diffusion of innovations. As we
have documented elsewhere (Blackler and Brown, 1978)
the task of promoting socio-technical theory was, in
later years, to become a prime concern of social
scientists impressed by it. By 1965, however, some
work had already been undertaken on this kind of issue
by Emery and Oeser (1958) who, working with concepts
developed by Kurt Lewin, had studied the diffusion of
new principles for farming in rural Australia. Later
(see Herbst, 1976) the applicability of the model
suggested by this research for the diffusion of social,
rather than technological, inventions was to be called
into doubt. Yet in the mid 1960's the Tavistock
workers were confident enough of their ideas in this
respect to use them to guide not only the change
process attempted in Shell but also to use it to guide
their work of introducing autonomous work groups to
Norwegian industry mentioned above. Reviewing the
latter project, Qvale has provided a neat summary of
the diffusion principles Tavistock people held in the
mid 1960's. These he states as

(a) Diffusion of new principles must start within the
     existing structure and in a way flow from one
     level of leaders to the next.

(b) Generally, external scientific advisors will only
     influence the diffusion process through the
     leaders.

(c) Oral and written communication is rarely enough
     to lead to change, except on the level of the
     leaders.

(d) Outside the level of the leaders diffusion depends
     upon the force of the example. In order to be
     effective the demonstration must be such that
     every one can see the similarity with his own

condition.

(e)   A well respected person or group must be behind
      the example.

Here, then, was a wide ranging and impressive range
of ideas that the Tavistock researchers were equipped
with when managers from Shell approached them for
help.   An analysis of social ills, a prescription for
their resolution by companies adopting new roles and
managing their affairs by new principles, a clearly
specified strategy for introducing changes by
influencing 'opinion leaders' and initiating
'demonstration projects', all these were combined to
form an impressive package.   This is then the
orientation brought to the Shell project by the
Tavistock workers.   They believed their work was
important and that their analysis of what the
circumstances in general demanded was certainly
applicable to Shell.   Given this confidence and
enthusiasm they were willingly to undertake a major
effort to convince Shell's managers of their position.
As we noted before the whole project presented itself
as a marvellous opportunity for them to try and put
their developing theories into action.

3 The Company

"NEW VALUES IN OLD BOTTLES" - WHY SHELL BECAME INVOLVED

Within the last decade notions of the imminent
emergence of a post-industrial society have become
increasingly debated in managerial as well as academic
circles. For example, a top manager of the Exxon
corporation has edited a book which centres upon 'the
conflict between a society that is changing rapidly and
a workplace that is not' (Rosow, 1973). And
Gyllenhammar (1977), in his discussion of the changes
in work organisation introduced within A.B. Volvo
states quite explicitly that such changes were a vital
part of the strategy of the organisation to move
towards a 'healthy human "post-industrial" society'
(p.164). However whether within Shell in 1965 the
prime motivation for engagement in the philosophy
programme was an acceptance of the inevitability of
post-industrial society, seems a matter of some dispute. For Trist (writing in the epilogue to Hill's
1971 book) it seemed clear that Shell's top management
held views very similar to his own. He writes:

> 'There was a strong likelihood, it seemed to
> us, that a number of (Shell's) key members had,
> through their own experience and in their own
> terms, reached conclusions similar to our own -
> otherwise Paul Hill would never have put
> forward the type of programme he had proposed
> and this would never have been accepted by the
> managing director and his senior colleagues
> after thorough discussion in a new type of
> conference about a new type of issue'. (p.196)

However elsewhere in Hill's book there are powerful
indications that the rationale for the company's
involvement was rather more immediately pragmatic.
Hill observes that by the early 1960's there was a
growing need to improve the company's existing

industrial relations practices. In particular five
factors were identified as contributing both to high
labour costs within the Shell UK refineries and a
pattern of 'crisis management' in the industrial
relations field. The pattern of union negotiations was
confused (operators were represented by one union which
negotiated at a national level, craftsmen by nine or
ten others which together negotiated locally) and a
leap frog pattern of wage claims had been typical.
Demarcation disputes were a major headache. Overtime
was worked excessively. Reduction, by natural wastage,
of wage earners had been resisted by the unions
although technical developments had made it
theoretically possible. Supervisors felt constant
concessions to shop stewards had eroded their
authority.

Commenting on this background Hill says:

> 'the problem of motivating people to work
> effectively - especially at shop-floor level -
> was of long standing in the company. The
> problem really started in the early 1950's,
> after the major plant expansions at Shell
> Haven and Stanlow. It seemed by the early
> 1960's still to be growing, particularly at
> Shell Haven. By then, the problem was
> threatening to assume for many people in
> supervisory roles an aspect of inevitability,
> something so deep rooted that it appeared
> it could never be solved'. (p.19)

Hill is, it should be pointed out, at pains to
demonstrate that this 'problem' was by no means unique
to Shell. Indeed senior managers who commented to us
strongly emphasised that compared to other industries
the industrial relations climate at that time within
Shell Refining was not at all bad, although scope for
improvement was recognised. Hill generalises this
theme in the introductory chapter to his book,
entitled 'The Motivation Problem in Industry', and
reviewing the growing incidents of strikes in Britain
between 1966 and 1970 he concludes:

'The picture that emerges demonstrates an
increasing number and a widening range of
people in the UK are experiencing discontent
with some aspect of their jobs; or to put it
in other terms, the problem of motivating
people in organisations to work effectively
and conscientiously is a growing one'.
(p.6, emphasis added)

This perspective - the perceived failure of
traditional management controls and the need to find
new ones - is reflected in the report Hill's E.R.P. (1)
Unit submitted to top management. Weekly paid
employees are not committed to company objectives, it
said, and in such a situation conventional bargaining
tactics are unlikely to be successful. 'Therefore'
the report continues,

'we should make it our long term policy to
secure a fundamental change in attitude on
the part of employees where, in a climate of
mutual trust and confidence between man and
management, it becomes possible for them to
commit themselves fully to the company
objective of having its work carried out
with maximum efficiency and productivity".
(p.43, emphasis added)

Committed people, the argument elaborates, are in any
case more likely to perform better than uncommitted
ones.

The report's clearly instrumental orientation
regarding other peoples attitudes and values continues
in the programme it proposes for changing their minds.
Before the attitudes of shop floor people could be
changed, it was suggested it would be necessary to
secure changes in attitudes amongst supervisors and
management. In particular, a 'participative' management and supervisory style was prescribed as necessary.

'Each boss should take his subordinates into
his confidence, encourage them to contribute

22

to and participate in any decisions which will
affect them or their work, help them to set
their own goals or targets and leave them free
to carry them out. In short, to make it
possible for them, with his guidance, to commit
themselves and their energies whole-heartedly
to the objectives of the company in the tasks
they undertake'. (p.44)

However, there is no doubting that this participation
is to be undertaken only within certain definite
constraints. The submission to top management
continues:

'It should perhaps be stressed that this
style by no means equates with "soft" management. The boss (at the appropriate level)
still takes the decisions. Indeed, this
system, whilst leading to true delegation
and the consequent more rapid development of
the subordinate, will also make weak links
or ineffective subordinates more conspicuous'.
(p.45)

In practical terms two approaches to this interpretation of the 'motivation problem' were proposed.
In the first place the intention was to change the
attitudes of managers, as a prelude to changing those
of shop floor people. To do this a draft statement of
objectives and company philosophy should be prepared
which, once top management approved it, should be
debated down the hierarchy of Shell Refining. The help
of social scientists was to be sought for this part of
the programme.

Second, the E.R.P. Unit proposed that ground should
be prepared for productivity bargains with the unions.
Study groups should explore implications of changes
the company wanted to introduce, working in preparation
for the deals, while the attitude change programme had
its effect (2). Later, the writers of the proposals
assumed, the attitude change programme and the
productivity deals would each be mutually supportive.

In March 1965 the managing director and the top
management group of Shell Refining in principle
accepted the diagnosis and action plan proposed by
Hill's unit, and themselves decided that a company
philosophy participative in style, as advocated in the
report, should be adopted by managers and supervisors
throughout the organisation.

It is therefore appropriate at this point to specify
in some detail the ambitious and comprehensive
formulation of the company philosophy. We reproduce
below a summary of its main points taken from Hill
(pp.57-59):

'1. Primary objectives. The company's primary
objective is expressed in terms of maximising
its contribution to the Group's long-term
profitability, insofar as this arises from
the efficient use of resources. There follows
what could be termed the company's social
objective:· this involves commitment to two
key concepts:-

(a) That all the resources it uses are
"social resources" (that is, are in
the last analysis resources of the
community), and must be protected and
developed as such.

(b) That the resources must be used to
contribute to the satisfaction of the
community's needs for products and
services.

Thus the company commits itself to seeking
improved profitability and the creation of
new wealth only in ways which will also
benefit society - through meeting community
needs efficiently and through protecting and
developing the social resources it uses.

2. Specific objectives. Six specific objectives
are spelled out, within the overall framework

of the primary objective. Two are operational
objectives, concerned with meeting present
and future market requirements. The third is
related to the company's position in the
Group. The last three derive from the
commitment to protect and develop resources
and are concerned with the development of
people, safety and the need to minimise
pollution of the environment.

3. The principle of joint optimisation as a
   guide to implementation. The guiding
   principle to assist the company in pursuing
   its objectives is the joint optimisation of
   the social and the technical systems. Joint
   optimisation means the best possible matching
   together of the people in any unit and the way
   their jobs are organised, with the physical
   equipment and material resources in that unit.
   The statement of this principle here leads on
   to an examination of the technical system,
   and of its implications for the design of the
   social system.

4. Key characteristics of the evolving technical
   system. Seven fundamental characteristics
   of the technical system are identified which
   are likely to remain unchanged in the forsee-
   able future, and which must therefore be
   taken into account in deciding how best to
   design the social system.

5. Implications for the social system. By
   considering the implications of the key
   technical characteristics, the most appropriate matching human characteristics are
   suggested. The most important human task
   in running process operations is identified
   as information handling. As this is a skill
   which cannot be controlled by external
   supervision, employees must be internally
   motivated to carry it out efficiently. It
   follows that the key human characteristics

required are responsibility and commitment.

6. Responsibility and commitment. This section
    is concerned with what must be done to create
    conditions in which people will develop
    responsibility and commitment to their tasks.
    It is suggested that two things are necessary:

    (a) Satisfactory terms and conditions of
         employment.

    (b) Jobs which enable them to satisfy the
         basic psychological needs of human
         beings in their work.

    What are considered to be the main
    psychological needs are then set out,
    together with some general principles to be
    taken into account in redesigning jobs.

7. Principle of implementation of the philosophy.
    The philosophy must be tested in the company
    through all employees having the opportunity
    to relate its implications to their own
    situation. Senior managers have a special
    responsibility for leading the process of
    testing and dissemination, and for
    implementation'.

THE PASSING OF AN ERA - HOW SHELL EMPLOYEES RECALL
REASONS FOR THE EXERCISE

From our interviews with people in Shell today who
recall the company philosophy exercise we have some
idea about what people affected by it thought it was
intended to achieve. 'We needed something' a senior
manager told us. 'The oil industry was past its
halcyon days'.

   The perspective that employees offer, on the one
hand, shows a greater sense of history than does Hill's
account and, on the other, demonstrates a greater sense

of continuity with the future than does Trist's. The
story we were told was of how times were changing for
the company and how some strategem was needed to cope.
We group the descriptions of changing times that we
heard under six headings.

(a)   Paternalism in the company

In the 1950's, we were told, Shell had a reputation of
being a successful company in a profitable business.
For sick and retired employees, especially, it was
regarded as a benevolent generous employer and Shell
was considered a good place to work. Yet, like many
companies at this time, its mode of organisation was
paternalistic/authoritarian. Differences in status
between salaried staff and weekly paid staff were
considerable. Attitudes to senior men were
deferential. Feelings about the propriety of
considerable differences between salaried and weekly
paid employees were changing however.

(b)   Changing attitudes towards industry

A more critical approach to industrial production was
beginning to influence public opinion (Ralph Nader is
the best known single campaigner of this era and there
were the early stirrings of a new ecological awareness
 e.g. Rachael Carson's 'Silent Spring').

(c)   Recent traumas in the oil industry

The oil business had recently become less profitable
than had previously been the case. The later 1950's
and early 1960's saw the Suez crisis and continuing
change in the Middle East with the emerging power of
OPEC. Several urgent attempts had been made to
improve efficiency within Shell (at Stanlow, for
example, productivity deals covering a restricted range
of items were signed in 1960 and 1963, a 'fair wages'
clause was signed around this time, and job evaluation
was introduced). It seems, though, that these efforts
had only restricted impact.

(d)   Industrial relations in the company

Paul Hill's account of the industrial relations climate
in the company at this time, to which we have already
referred was echoed in stories we were told of a
history of demarcation disputes stretching back into
the 1950's, of the tendency for industrial relations
disputes to snowball from one area to another, of a
tradition of excessive overtime being worked, of a
difficult to administer multi-grade wage structure and
of problems regarding comparative wages with
contractors used in the refineries. While, as we have
seen Hill's E.R.P. Unit was to diagnose these problems
and propose a specific plan of productivity deals to
cope with these, other people also were wondering what
could be done. 'Something was in the air' we were
told. (Indeed at Stanlow, working quite independently
of the E.R.P. Unit, we heard how a manager charged
with considering possibilities for a labour deal for
1965 had in two weeks produced a series of proposals
for management consideration that with only minor
modification, he did not envisage a system of no
payment for overtime, was exactly what was achieved in
the next four years).

(e)   Activities of competitors

Against the background of a far more competitive oil
industry and problematic industrial relations was the
belief that Shell's competitors were gaining strength.
In particular Esso, the company's keenest rival, was
known to have negotiated further reaching productivity
deals (reported in Flanders, 1964) than had been
possible in Shell.

(f)   The results of a demanning exercise

Around this time in Houston, Texas efforts to keep
open a refinery during a strike amongst its operators
had been successful and indicated, to a now very jumpy
and cost conscious industry, that refineries could be
kept running with significantly less personnel than
hitherto had been believed. Subsequently, manpower

surveys were to be undertaken and Shell's UK refineries were to be told they were about 20% overmanned. Here then, in a company keen to review its industrial relations practices, seemed a way of making savings so anxiously sought.

   In fact in July 1962 an announcement had been made that was to fore-shadow the subsequent rundown. At Stanlow a bulletin entitled 'Your Job with Shell. What Lies Ahead' began by recalling the increased competition of the oil business and the refinery's efforts to increase efficiency. It stated that in recent years costs had been prevented from rising while wages and salaries had increased. Redundancies however, it was emphasised, had up till then been avoided. Plans, the details of which were not mentioned, for further improvements were promised, before it was concluded:

      'It is not always right to assume that joining Shell at Stanlow means a job for life, although we want it to work out that way. We expect to get a fair day's work for a fair day's pay and if there are individuals who are not prepared to keep their part of the bargain, they will find as always that we have no place for them.

      Some will wonder what will happen to a man whose job disappears. We go to a lot of trouble to fit people into other suitable jobs, as some of you will know. It sometimes take time, but it nearly always works out.

      Apart from this, there may arise general trading or economic difficulties which could be caused either by general world conditions or our inability to be competitive. If we should have to stop some of our activities we would certainly expect to deal with the resulting situation in the manner outlined above'.

   Subsequently we were told a bad atmosphere developed in the refineries. Overtime bans, mass meetings, poor

morale followed. In the event the redundancy programme
that materialised in 1964 was a voluntary scheme for
unionised people, but a compulsory one for non-
unionised staff. (The latter received a larger
severance payment). Insecurity was experienced.
Weekly paid staff saw well respected people leaving.
Supervisors (who were not unionised) were particularly
at risk. Some of these felt let down, blaming any
poor performance on their part on what they felt had
been erosions in their authority. It was felt too that
staff appraisals had not been honest enough in previous
years, and that the consequent lack of prior warning
meant that some of the supervisors who were sacked were
'shattered and bitter'. Those who felt they had just
survived remained insecure. Others were startled by
the suddenness of it all, and some middle managers
later were to express deep bitterness at a lack of
consultation in the way redundancies had been imposed.

Of the people we spoke to about these times one did
remark on the benefits that the 1964 scheme had for
the company. He suggested that, apart from the savings
on wages and salaries, people were alerted to the
changing situation of the company and that some less
capable staff were severed. Yet, in our experience,
compliments for the programme were not easy to find.
The legacy of cynicism left by it is predominant in
peoples minds. A manager associated with the actual
administration of the rundown told us:

> 'It left a nasty taste in my mouth. I
> resolved then never to have anything to do
> with such a thing again. I will never live
> down my involvement in it. People still
> remember'.

Indeed, a legacy of mistrust towards the Company can
be found amongst some longer serving employees, from
the union representative who dates his concern to
negotiate a 'security of employment' clause from this
period, to the middle manager and self styled 'company
man' ('like Blackpool rock I've got the words "Shell
employee" stamped right through me') who nonetheless

said of the company, 'My experience is that as the economic gloom gets worse "they" lash out more and more'. Nowadays, there is a feeling that natural wastage might have achieved the same number of employee reductions at Stanlow (though not at Shell Haven), and that with hindsight, although the refineries were overmanned, the programme was ill thought out anyway. (Within a year the company were recruiting once again. Some of those previously severed were taken back, though it was commented to us rather sadly by a junior level manager at Stanlow: 'We lost good men, then got a rabble back who had since soured our industrial relations scene with their vicious and extreme militancy').

We must however note that whilst the majority of our respondents were highly critical of this episode, alternative interpretations do exist. Especially amongst members of the management team responsible for the exercise, it is felt that the trauma was over-exaggerated as one of the managers of the rundown put it to us: 'We had to put the blocks on to stop people rushing to the gates .... at Stanlow everyone leaving except one person out of more than fifty were all delighted to leave - they all had jobs to go to'.

Paul Hill does record in his book that this rundown took place. He lists some benefits that he believed followed from it - numbers were reduced now, so longer term planning on this was not necessary, a 'first break in the web of restrictive practices' was made, the idea that a job in Shell was one for life was demolished so it had 'prepared people for further changes in the future'. Also, he records 'problems' - upset morale, resentment at lack of consultation and the fact that non-unionised people were treated differently for unionised ones, increased mistrust of management's motives (he especially nominates the craftsmen's shop stewards at Shell Haven) and the demolition of 'the tradition of loyalty to the company, which had provided a form of motivation, a sense of obligation to do a fair day's work'. (p.25, emphasis added)

31

Yet an awareness of the bad feelings associated with this period is essential to an understanding of the place of the philosophy exercise in the company. First, there are the reactions to the philosophy exercise that people were to feel in the light of the rundown in staff. While it is true that Hill's unit itself was not behind both the philosophy and the rundown, rightly or wrongly, a connection was to be seen. (We document in more detail later how people responded to the philosophy itself). Hill is correct, we believe, when he says that old traditions within the company had been demolished, although it does not seem to us that he understood fully the significance of this context for how his philosophy exercise was later received.

Second, of course, were the consequences of the rundown for the subsequently enhanced 'motivation problem' that management faced. We do not know precisely how aware senior management was of the effect its policies had had. There seems little doubt that the resentment of more junior status people was fairly unmistakable although it may be that the resentment of more middle managers was not fully appreciated. Yet Hill's proposals for initiating a new deal of partnership and co-operation must, in 1965, have seemed too good to be missed. As one of our interviewees euphemistically put it: 'It was realised that the rundown in staff had not been too tactful'.

THE VARYING ACCOUNTS

In these last two chapters we have seen how the accounts of employees today, of the E.R.P. Unit and of the Tavistock Institute differ in their understandings of the reasons for the company philosophy.

The various positions that we have described can be summarised as follows. For the Tavistock there was the opportunity to draft a statement of what they felt was the new and emerging role for Shell (and, by implication, organisations) in the modern world. A role characterised more by collaboration than by

competition had to be articulated. There was also the
opportunity to see how soon people might come to adopt
new, and supposedly more appropriate, values.

   For the E.R.P. Unit there was the challenge of trying
to introduce a new approach to management based on
recent social science views that emphasised the trust-
worthiness of human nature. An industrial relations
problem in the company, born of inconvenient attitudes
of shop floor people, was the nub of the issue for the
E.R.P. group. To cope with it, management approaches
to people at the interpersonal level were to be
modified in a 'human relations' approach and a new
philosophy of management was to be debated throughout
the company.

   The picture we constructed from employees
recollections nowadays of the philosophy exercise,
contains, with the sobriety of twelve years hindsight,
a stronger sense of the historical context than Hill's
account does, and a stronger sense of continuity into
the future than does Trist's. According to this
picture the company needed above all to restore the
legitimacy and efficacy of management's call to
collective effort. Faced by difficult business
conditions and industrial relations problems the
company had confounded its position with a major
redundancy programme. On this view, while the
philosophy talked the language of 'psychological needs'
there was no philanthropy in it; it was strictly a
pragmatic development in response to a difficult
problem for managers.

   The comparisons and differences between these views
are fascinating. At first sight Trist seems the odd
one out. He assumes a changing rationale for
organisations in society. Hill, on the other hand, has
as his starting point the need to change shop floor
people's attitudes. Employees today, while as we will
see some found the concepts within the philosophy
exciting and others found the exercise objectionable,
agree pretty well with Hill on the state of affairs
at that time.

Trist's view differs in another important respect
from Hill's. His vision of turbulent environments,
places, it seems, somewhat more faith in the
spontaneous power of trust in and respect of others in
helping to create order out of chaos than does Hill.
From our reading of his book we think it would be wrong
to say Hill tries to conceal this, his point is that
the 'techniques' of trust and involvement are more
successful than alternative approaches born of mistrust.

Yet these differences should not be allowed to
conceal the similarities between Hill's and Trist's
views. As with other approaches culled from system's
theory, Trist's analysis does tend to conceive of
things from the point of view of how organisations may
best manage their affairs. Accordingly, it easily
leads to a managerial orientation; its implicit
priorities, (survival, adjustment, consensus, growth)
have much in common with managerial priorities. This,
we believe, accounts for the attractiveness of the
Tavistock approach to the E.R.P. Unit and later to some
managers. On the other hand, though, we argue later
that the differences we have documented between the
Tavistock's and Hill's orientations laid the basis for
some of the disappointments that were subsequently to
be associated with the scheme.

In contrast to the Hill and the Tavistock approaches
are the accounts of employees today. Hill and Trist
firmly write as people who are 'arranging the
organising'. These other accounts were related by
people aware it was they who were the ones 'being
organised'. Indeed, while the differing interests of
the Tavistock people and the E.R.P. Unit came together
in the shared excitement of a pioneering venture, the
responses of people who were the target of this venture
were very much more variable. In the next three
chapters we attempt to reconstruct what these responses
were.

NOTES

(1) 'Employee Relations Planning' Unit, set up in
     Shell Refining in 1963 to 'produce long term
     plans for dealing with the problems at shop
     floor level'.

(2) Staff status for hourly paid employees, annual
     salaries in place of hourly rates, no overtime
     payments, more flexibility and less demarcation,
     these were the areas envisaged by Hill's unit
     when its overall plan was proposed in 1965. Some
     four years later, the productivity deals as signed
     covered exactly these areas.

PART II

METHODS OF IMPLEMENTATION

4   Initial Reception of the Philosophy

Over an intensive two year period between 1965 and 1967 the philosophy was introduced to people in the Company. A brief outline of events in this period is as follows.

1965 March   Top management (as we have seen) approve the E.R.P. Unit's initial report and endorse its recommendations. They decide a philosophy should be drawn up.

1965 October   By now the Tavistock Institute and the E.R.P. Unit have drawn up a draft philosophy statement.

                  With the E.R.P. and Tavistock people present as advisors, top management debate the philosophy at a three day conference. A programme of further dissemination, to senior staff, is approved.

1966 March   By this date 270 senior staff across the organisation (including some at head office) have attended a philosophy conference. These were $2\frac{1}{2}$ day residential events involving about twenty people from the same location, normally with at least two people from the Tavistock and two from E.R.P. Each was chaired by the appropriate refinery manager or his deputy.

At this time progress is reviewed by
the top management who decide

(a)   further modifications of the
       philosophy statement to cease for
       twelve months (amendments had been
       proposed by some of the
       conferences)

(b)   dissemination to continue,
       ultimately to involve foremen and
       hourly paid people

(c)   Union officials and shop stewards
       to be involved

(d)   Some further measures to be
       introduced, including (pilot) job
       redesign projects, and joint
       working parties (of management
       and worker representatives).

1966 September   A second phase of shorter residential
                  conferences at Stanlow continues till
                  around now. Foremen and supervisors
                  have been involved, and a few special
                  conferences were arranged for union
                  officials and shop stewards. (Fewer
                  Tavistock and E.R.P. people were
                  involved in running these conferences).
                  From now on departmental discussion
                  groups were to be the vehicle for
                  introducing the philosophy to hourly
                  paid people.

1967 March   At Shell Haven a second phase of (non-
                  residential) conferences continues till
                  about this date. Shop stewards were
                  included in the conferences for other
                  staff. A series of conferences for
                  junior and a proportion of hourly paid
                  staff were run, and one-third of
                  hourly paid people were thus involved.

> From now on departmental discussions
> were the vehicle for continuing to
> involve people.

Hill's account of this series of events contains
much useful detail on what was debated at the
conferences, what decisions were taken and when and
what procedures were followed at the meetings.
Crucially also, he makes a number of observations
about how the exercise was being received.

The account we have collated below of people's
recollections of the exercise are of much interest,
providing as they do a different perspective on the
events than does Hill's account. In some respects
certainly they do corroborate his interpretation of
events. But it has to be said that in a number of
other aspects this is not the case.

THE OCTOBER 1965 CONFERENCE AT WHICH TOP MANAGEMENT
APPROVE THE PHILOSOPHY

(a)   As described in Hill's book

Trist says of this conference which introduced the
philosophy to Shell UK's most senior managers, that it
'was an intense experience, intellectually and
emotionally, for all who participated' (in Hill,
op. cit., p.199). Hill states:

> 'The outcome was that each manager present
> accepted the document as valid and appropriate
> to the company's needs. Each gave his commit-
> ment to manage in accordance with its principles.
> It was felt it contained objectives from which
> a positive and stable philosophy of management
> had been derived and offered the means of
> releasing unused human capabilities and of
> improving motivation and commitment. The level
> of enthusiasm varied and some reservations
> were expressed but overall there was strong

support for the statement. One manager
considered this event could well prove to be
the most important conference the company
had ever had. The managing director made
clear his support of the principles and said
that the three days' test out of the document
had dispelled some initial scepticism. He
then stated his personal commitment'. (p.76)

Reservations, Hill says, concerned mainly the
problem of how the philosophy might be disseminated
throughout the Company, and how it could be put into
practice. He includes a lot of detail concerning how
the philosophy statement was explained and debated.

Subsequently, the manager of Stanlow (henceforth we
refer to him as 'manager A') is described as keen to
begin discussing the document with his own management
team, confident, it seems, of its acceptability. The
manager at Shell Haven ('manager B') and his deputy
wished, in Hill's words,

'to move more slowly and not rush into their
first conference. Confronted by a long-
standing industrial relations problem at the
refinery, and a relatively poor level of
morale, they wanted to be sure their senior
staff were committed to the contents of a
draft statement before time was spent
considering implementation possibilities'. (p.81)

(b) As recalled today

We were fortunate enough in speaking to the one top
manager remaining in Shell who was present at this
conference. His account provides a somewhat
different perspective. At the time of the conference
he was one of the managers from the Shell Haven
refinery.

'When I went to this conference I wondered why
so much emphasis was being placed on words, on
the subtleties of meaning. I found the
terminology very confusing. There was a lot
of jargon from the Tavistock people. I
wondered how they could help. What was new
here? In retrospect it is clear to me there
was a lot that was new, but that was not how
it seemed at the time.

Manager A was very committed. But we (at Shell
Haven) were never so sure. I could not myself
divorce what I was listening to from my own
personality. I had been a task centred man, by
background, upbringing. In the back-end of
1965 I was having difficulties thinking about
changing my approach. I couldn't see any
failing in it. In my thirteen years with the
company I had risen to a senior position.
What was wrong with that?

My boss, manager B, was a very intellectual
man. At this stage he enjoyed the debate with
the Tavistock people. But he didn't see any
need to change. He was confident of his
ability, his powers of logic. He did not feel
any need to consult.

So we were a long way from the conviction of
manager A.

But we felt we had to do something. The ideas
had been sold well to the boss of manufacturing.
We had to do something as the top man wanted
to go this way. Given a free choice I'm not
sure what we would have done!

We were more sluggish getting off the mark
than Stanlow was. We weren't sure how to
handle it. We had the Tavistock people over
for a few days but I blew my top at them!
They wouldn't give us an opinion as what we

ought to do. "What are we paying for?", I
exploded! They explained they were working
only as catalysts and we had to take
responsibility for any programme. I learned
a lot from that.

But after this conference we were sluggish.
We were not as sure of ourselves as manager A.
We thought he was racing. Also if it was to
continue, we knew we didn't want to be too
dependent on the Tavistock'.

While we have no other personal recollections of
people present at this conference to present,
numerous comments by people we spoke to at Stanlow
confirm the extent to which manager A at least was
committed to the philosophy.

Two senior managers (neither of whom particularly
sympathise with manager A in this respect) commented:

'It was a moral crusade for him, as if he
had had a conversion on the road to Damascus.
The company philosophy, then the productivity
deal, job enrichment, organisation development
were all part of this crusade. He was a very
gifted man. But you had to believe.

He was a humane sort of person, an idealist.
He believed in better working relationships.
He wanted to create an attitude of bonhomie
and goodwill. He deeply believed that overtime and wage structures as we had them then
were morally wrong and should be thought out
again'.

Comments from people at that time in junior
managerial positions add to the picture of a
proselyte:

'We needed something to counter the doldrums
which followed the 1964 rundown. But the

philosophy itself would not have happened
except for manager A. What the refinery
manager thinks is very important.

Manager A was a man of principle. He
believed in involvement, the potential of
people to respond. He pushed the philosophy
very very hard.

I relate the whole thing to Manager A. But
there were a number of people who, in the short
term, always pointed to the philosophy. They
were trying to follow. These people were
trying to "set fire" to the refinery!'

THE PROGRAMME OF CONFERENCES, OCTOBER 1965 -
MARCH 1967

(a) As described in Hill's book

A series of conferences was planned after top
management had approved the philosophy with the
intention of involving all employees, including
weekly paid staff. Details of how they were to be
run was left to each location to arrange, although
senior management were always the first to be
involved (their acceptance was first deemed
necessary if the programme was to continue). All
salaried staff were included in the conference
programme. At Shell Haven, after one-third of the
weekly paid staff (including shop stewards) had been
included, the vehicle for further dissemination
became departmental meetings. At Stanlow this was
the method adopted to reach all the weekly paid
staff, except for some shop stewards who were
involved in special conferences for them.

   Hill provides some indications of how the early
conferences for senior refinery managers progressed:
the role of profits, and the predominance of
technical over social considerations was especially
discussed at Stanlow, the degree of commitment of

45

top management to the philosophy (following their staff rundown) at Shell Haven.

Of the effects of the conferences in general he states his opinion (p.92) that while understanding and commitment to the philosophy varied (with a small minority enthusiastic and anxious to implement it, and another small minority 'refusing to believe' the company intended to put it into effect) in general 'the conferences achieved their objectives of imparting an understanding of the philosophy statement and of its implications for the way the company should run its affairs to achieve the best results'.

Hill also summarises the reactions of the Tavistock and E.R.P. people who, through their involvement at the conferences 'were able to gain good overall impression of the dissemination process'. Of them Hill says (and we quote in full):

'They were struck with the way in which the document served to generate a wealth of different reactions and encouraged many people at all levels to speak their minds openly. They were impressed at the serious- ness with which people discussed the issues raised by the statement and the importance they clearly attributed to them. There was no suggestion that people thought they were playing games. They were impressed also with the great enthusiasm of some conference members, particularly at Stanlow, and their determination to push the programme forward. It seemed clear that the content of the statement was responding to a real need felt by many people in the organisation'. (p.92)

Three less satisfactory aspects are mentioned by Hill. A feeling that expectations had been lifted high and disillusionment might follow if things were not seen to move on. A worry expressed by people that the Royal Dutch Shell group (of which the Shell

UK refinery capacity was only about 10%) might not fully support the programme. A doubt that some people simply saw the philosophy as a plea to 'be nice to people'. 'However' Hill observes 'the verdict on the general outcome of the conference dissemination process must be that it was very successful'.

(b) As recalled today

At both Stanlow and Shell Haven we met two people who had been at the early conferences in the series, those for senior managers in the refineries.

Of the two at Stanlow, one recalls how much manager A liked the philosophy and the enthusiasm he showed. To the best of his recollection, 'broadly speaking the document was accepted by people present'. The other was rather more critical in his recollections:

> 'There was a genuine discussion of the document at that stage, it was later to become more of a selling exercise for the junior staff but early on many senior people became involved. At this time I thought the document was going to be refined, have wide distribution, be distributed to shareholders with a definitive version perhaps being published. So I took it seriously. It was only later that I realised that this so-called "philosophy" was just bits of paper, an "Aunt Sally" for internal consumption only. I suppose it was put up to solve these morale problems and in that respect I suppose it was convenient and successful.
>
> I saw the first form of it. Had the Tavistock written it do you know? As a vehicle for discussion it was disastrous. There was no reference to profit! When you read it very closely the emphasis you would pick up was on benevolence to the poor hard worked employee! It created the wrong impression.

The thing that sticks in my mind now was this thing about profit. There were only three of us who stood up and argued about the importance of profit. I was amazed.

The meeting itself was well structured. That was thanks to the Tavistock people. But at the conference there were two kinds of people. There were those who thought they were being brainwashed. And the rest were being high minded, they thought it was a good thing to do anyway'.

Of the two people at Shell Haven that we spoke to who recall the early philosophy discussions, both spoke of the brewing resentment there of the 1964 rundown and how it coloured events.

One recalled how, with the assistance of the Tavistock people, he had been encouraged to speak out on the matter. It was an emotional experience he would not forget. He recalls how he then felt feelings of bitterness towards his colleagues who did not speak up also.

The other (whom we quoted as being present at the earlier conference for top management) attended as a representative of top management. Some people, he remembered, participated very well. Others were silent, one in particular 'not saying a word' for the whole $2\frac{1}{2}$ day period. Expressions of resentment about the '64 rundown came as a shock to the top managers it seems as perhaps for the first time they realised they had not had the backing of their senior and middle managers in it.

Leaving now the early conferences for senior managers other people we spoke to had attended one or more of the many later conferences held to disseminate the philosophy. Not including union representatives or shop stewards (we discuss what they told us later) twelve of those we spoke to at Stanlow and four of those at Shell Haven had attended them.

From accounts of these conferences we have been able
to reconstruct certain aspects of what seemed to take
place in them, that adds a dimension absent from
Hill's account. In a number of respects what we were
told consistently fell into a pattern. This was true
whether the accounts of these conferences was
provided by people uniquely placed, by virtue of their
involvement then in running the conferences and later
by their continued involvement in personnel or related
work at the same locations, or by others who simply
recalled their own reactions or described their
recollection of 'the spirit of the times'. In the
following presentation we try and reconstruct this
pattern.

We begin by reproducing the recollections of two
people, one at Shell Haven and one at Stanlow, who
assisted by people from E.R.P. and/or the Tavistock
Institute, helped organise a number of the conferences.
Their opinions of these events now are directly
comparable to the reaction then of the E.R.P. and
Tavistock people that, as we have seen, Hill relies
on.

The first, a manager at Shell Haven, describes in
this quotation from the interview he gave us the
basic position argued in the philosophy document.
He then speculates about the extent of people's
actual (as against apparent) commitment to it.

    'The whole basis was, what business are we in?
    What is the philosophy of the company? "We
    are here to make a profit", that was basically
    (what we called) Position I. "We are here to
    make a profit, but realising there are social
    constraints of society and employees which
    will impose a limit on our profits". That was
    Position II. And Position III was: "We are
    custodians of the assets of society and we may
    not even make profits at its expense". The
    implication being you had to be successful at
    making profits but within that framework, and I
    wondered in retrospect whether that was understood.

According to Positions I, II and III there would
be some overall and specific objectives which
recognise the characteristics of the oil
industry, and certain kinds of recognisable
actions to meet these.

So, the first thing to debate was, do we
believe that Position III (or II, or I) is what
we are in and where we should be?

Now that's where I believe that however many
hands went up the consensus was never more than
Position $2\frac{1}{2}$, perhaps only Position 2.1! But
we all said we believed in Position III ....

I would put it this way. There were probably
50% who really wanted to make Position III a
go and thought they could. There were 25% who
would like to but didn't think it had much
hope. And there were 25% who didn't think it
was right anyway, but weren't going to say so
.... although you had better not take this as
literally as I have said it'.

This respondent emphasised to us that at the time
of the conferences he would have presented a more
optimistic assessment but that with the benefit of
hindsight these percentages represented a more
realistic assessment.

The second manager we quote here helped run many
of the conferences for people in the Stanlow refinery.
In what follows, he speculates about the extent to
which people there fully understood the concept of
the 'Joint Optimisation' of the social and technical
systems which was, of course, the second key element
in the philosophy statement.

'Looking back I would say that really only
about 5% of the people who attended the
conferences really understood it. Manager A
kept saying "It is not a 'be nice' policy, but
it is a philosophy for getting the best out of

50

people". But the idea of Joint Optimisation was not really understood. Engineers could not grasp the idea of optimising what can't be measured!

It actually did become a "be nice to people" philosophy I suppose. Then later on when Manager A retired, there was a rumour he was studying for a degree in social work or something similar. This confirmed the image of "being nice" in people's minds ....

If you mention the notion of Joint Optimisation now, you get a snort of laughter'.

Here then, are two people uniquely placed to pass judgement. (Both were involved in the dissemination conferences, both still find much that is important and relevant in the philosophy itself, both are now working in the same refineries today as they were then, one has always remained in the personnel field, the other has mostly been in this kind of work). Yet, exact figures aside, one says about half the people at these conferences could not accept the fundamental position in the philosophy though everyone said they did. The other that only a fraction of the people present even understood its second most basic idea. This hardly sounds like the 'very successful' programme that Hill refers to!

If all this retrospective analysis is true then the question arises as to how the E.R.P. and the Tavistock team became convinced during the conference programme that all was going well. (1) Being partial through their involvement, of course, one might argue they were not themselves the best authorities at the time to judge the efficiency of their own work. The first of the managers whom we have just quoted makes some further observations which are relevant however. We asked, why did people say they went along with 'Position III' if they did not agree with it?

'If you go along to one of Billy Graham's
meetings and you're the only one who hasn't
gone down to be saved, do you think you can
sit there? They were, I would think, a bit
like that. I mean it wasn't revivalist. But
that was the pressure. That's what I meant
when I said "hands went up" ' .

Where then was this pressure coming from?

'I would think the pressure, I would certainly
like to think this, the pressure was from
people who felt, like me, that this was good
stuff, this was right, this was the long term
thing to do!'

While it would be fair to say that this was the only
time any of the people we spoke to about the
conferences described the pressures on people in quite
such terms, other similar observations were made to us.
Two other people associated with running the
conferences, one at that time with the E.R.P. Unit
the other the Tavistock Institute, agreed that while
dissent was discussed its persistence was not fully
recognised as legitimate. It does seem that
expressions of disagreement with the philosophy
tended to be given the status of 'problems' that
people were having with it, rather than being
regarded as statements of equally valid alternatives.

The euphoria which seems to have characterised some
of these conferences is perhaps illustrated in this
recollection by a (then) shift supervisor:

'Most of us found it very convincing. We felt
it was good, it could be a very good thing.
The bit about responsibility to the community
was sensible you know. And there were some
good ideas coming out of it, like no clocking
on, and the idea we are all professional people.
Remember Shell used to be paternalistic, anti-
union.

'In those days the "boss man" counted. But
at the conference they said "You call me
Eddie, I'll call you Jack". We thought, what
the bloody hell is going on here? But it made
you feel good. Then we all got drunk'.

And some people did pay tribute to the educational
value of the conferences commenting on how they had
found them useful in helping them clarify their roles,
how it was useful for managers to meet in less formal
conditions, how they picked up new ideas. The
conferences 'let a lot of air into the system' it was
said.

Yet the truth was that complimentary remarks about
the conferences were seldom made to us. A plant
manager, who was later to cooperate with the
Tavistock Institute in running an experiment in job
redesign at Stanlow and who described himself as
being 'a missionary at that time - I took it very
seriously - I had the zeal of a Jesuit!' said that
at the conference he attended:

'Views varied from people being very
enthusiastic - and for some there were careers
to be made out of all this - to those who
thought "bullshit". Most people were open
minded or waiting to see which way to jump.
But there was, no doubt, a genuine management
commitment and a feeling we could achieve a
lot'.

Other people commented also that junior management
people and below were far less likely to be convinced
than senior people. A (then) supervisor said:

'There was a range of views at all levels.
But management viewed it with more favour.
At the lower levels there was less interest
and understanding. For them, or many of
them, it was just a booze up'.

Indeed while it is undoubtedly true that the hopes, imaginations and expectations of some people were raised (one manager, himself committed to the philosophy at that time and respectful of it today, talked of the 'Elysian field' expectations that people had of the prospects for job redesign) for others this was certainly not so. Talk of 'brain-washing' was frequent. Here are three comments from (at that time) a section head at Stanlow, a clerk at Shell Haven, and a shift supervisor at Stanlow.

The Section Head:

'How did I feel at that time? The ideals, then, were above my head. All I was interested in was how it affected my section, what I could get out of it. I came away with the feeling I got nothing out of it. It was not presented at a low enough level.

There was a lot of mistrust at that level of management. What was the need for it? Was there something to be found? Is the mileage that we are putting in not adequate? I suppose it was done to provide a spurt via a rest-cure holiday. Generally it was not accepted by people at that level.

There was a feeling it was brainwashing. It did not reduce the barriers between management and the rest. In fact, it did exactly the opposite. It led to a polarisation'.

The Clerk:

'I don't want to be too rude about it. But it was gobbledegoop philosophy. I wondered what was going on. It felt like a propaganda exercise. It was a very complicated document. We were being told to work harder as the company needed to be more efficient. Well, we didn't resent that message so much as the method they used to tell us it. It was long-winded and expensive. It was brainwashing'.

The Shift Supervisor:

'A little bit must stick whatever you feel at the time. I don't remember what I thought was good but I was not very impressed. The general reaction of people was "It's a bit of a giggle". The only enthusiastic people there, were the lecturers. Possibly other people were enthusiastic but I didn't meet any.

We were there for a purpose. We were being indoctrinated on the role of Shell in the community, to shareholders, to employees. Some of the ideas were good but whether they are ever followed up when you get back from these courses is questionable.

I was suspicious because the 1964 "Golden Handshake" had been preceeded by consultants doing something, and other company exercises were followed by reductions'.

At the conclusion of the philosophy dissemination programme (September 1966 at Stanlow, March 1967 at Shell Haven) it was intended that shop floor level employees should be involved by discussions held in departmental meetings. We take up this part of the story in the next chapter

THE REACTIONS OF THE UNIONS

(a) As described in Hill's book

To complete this picture of people's recollections of their reactions to the launching of the philosophy, some mention of the responses of union officials and shop stewards is necessary.

55

It was important for the success of E.R.P.'s operation that the unions did not refuse to cooperate with the working parties that management were to propose to prepare the way for productivity deals. Also, following the big launch of the philosophy exercise, it was felt important that things should seem to continue and a number of 'pilot' job redesign projects were planned. Union consent was to be sought for these also.

Hill devotes a chapter in his book to describing conferences held specially for union officials and then for shop stewards at Stanlow, and describing the reactions of stewards at Shell Haven who had been included in the conferences there run for managers.

The picture he paints is of a highly successful operation. Management did have doubts about the likely reaction they were to meet but Hill is able to conclude:

> 'with the exception of the small but
> influential group of senior craft shop
> stewards at Shell Haven, and perhaps one or
> two individual officers at Stanlow, the
> general reaction of trade union representatives
> to the company's development programme was
> highly encouraging. In general, the two major
> implications which emerged for these were
> welcomed: namely, the company's intention to
> develop people's potentialities and build
> more satisfying jobs, and the intention to
> rationalise terms and conditions of employment
> so that, among other things, their members
> would enjoy a more stable level of income'.
> (p.104)

Union officials at Stanlow were sympathetic, some shop stewards there were very enthusiastic, a new era of openness and frankness between unions and management is portrayed as beginning in June 1966. Stanlow management and stewards issued a joint bulletin

publicising the stewards' intent to support the
philosophy, announcing experimental job redesign
projects were to start, the setting up of joint
working parties, and training schemes for all levels
of employees to aid their development. Later a party
of managers, union officials and shop stewards were,
with the Tavistock's guidance, to visit Norway to
meet people involved with Tavistock influenced job
redesign projects there.

At Shell Haven reactions were more mixed. Shop
stewards representing operators were mostly in favour
it seems, the senior stewards being very enthusiastic.
On the other hand senior stewards representing
craftsmen did not believe the company intended to put
the philosophy into practice, and remained suspicious
of the company's motives. Hill suggests these
particular stewards appeared to be unrepresentative of
practically all the craftsmen who attended Shell Haven
conferences in this respect.

(b)   As recalled today

At both Stanlow and Shell Haven we spoke to two people
each closely involved in these affairs. At Stanlow,
to a full time official of the operators' union and a
senior steward on the negotiating committee for
craftsmen. At Shell Haven we spoke to the (then)
vice-chairman of the operators' union and also a
senior steward on the craftsmens' negotiating
committee there.

A full time official at Stanlow recalled that the
purpose of the conference was to acquaint officials
with the company's philosophy and intentions. He
discussed the idea of people becoming involved in
their work and how someone overheard it being said
that 'it works in Norway'. The trip there to confirm
this, was enjoyable enough but unconvincing he said,
because Norwegian people have a different tradition
and do not mind working in self-managed groups.

57

The shop steward at Stanlow also felt the Norwegian trip was irrelevant, mentioning the fact that the demonstration projects there were not in the oil industry. He recalled rather more about his conference. It was useful in terms of hearing what the company philosophy meant but there was, he said, a feeling 'we were being softened up'. He thought the company was genuine about the philosophy. He recalled the attitude of full time officials at being one of 'suck it and see'.

The ex-vice chairman of the operators' union at Shell Haven had not, despite his position, attended a philosophy conference. He felt, though, that the spectre of a possible company rundown following the exercise made people sceptical.

The craft shop steward recalled the conference he attended as an informal social occasion. There was, he said, a lot of sniping from both sides. 'A hell of a lot that was said was tongue in cheek. What was being said was idealism. But the system does not give to idealism'. As he recalled, the company was seeking increased productivity through the philosophy, but would give no guarantees regarding effects on manning requirements, or rewards for increased effort. So for him the idea never got off the ground. He recalled, though, that morale was high because the company was making this sustained effort to improve industrial relations. 'People wanted to be convinced, you know'.

NOTES

(1) Not only was this, according to Hill, true for
     the regular members of the Tavistock team. A
     number of distinguished academics who visited
     the Tavistock Institute at this period including
     Lou Davis, Godfrey Gardner, Stanley Seashore,
     Martin Lakin and Hans van Beinum who helped at
     the dissemination conferences. Of this who's
     who? in the behavioural science world Hill says
     'they were able to look critically at the whole
     approach from close quarters and it was note-
     worthy that they were without exception impressed
     with its scope and originality'. (p.89)

5   Job Redesign and Managers as Change Agents

It was never intended that the philosophy conferences
should be regarded as ends in themselves. In the
minds of E.R.P. and the Tavistock they were just the
beginning. Real advances, it was thought, would come
later as the theoretical implications of the ideas
were to be turned into practice.

   Where were the advances to come? Hill (op.cit.)
lists four 'main channels of implementation' that
were to emerge. The first two we consider in this
chapter, the second two in the subsequent one. They
are:

(1)   Demonstration job redesign projects to illustrate
      the power of joint optimisation as an approach.

(2)   Departmental managers to act as centres for
      implementation. Especially, they were to
      disseminate the philosophy statement itself,
      introduce more participative approaches, and put
      the ideas of joint optimisation into practice.

(3)   Joint working parties of management and worker
      representatives together to explore new ways of
      working as a basis for productivity deals.

(4)   The principles of joint optimisation were to be
      incorporated in the design of a new refinery at
      Teesport.

   It is interesting to compare these 'main channels
of implementation' with the content of the philosophy
itself, and with the original intentions of its
architects. Centred around the concept of 'stewardship' (i.e. that the company 'is the custodian of the

assets of society and should not even make a profit at its expense') it certainly is true that the ideas of participative management and of 'joint optimisation' were considered to be important ways in which the philosophy could be acted out. Indeed the four main channels of implementation just listed exclusively emphasise the importance of such methods.

Conceivably,. however, other important ways should also be found of the company's 'stewardship' was to be well conducted. Hill himself, for example, (p.70) mentions concern for the company's appropriate treatment of materials, money and the environment. This concept of stewardship, to which we shall return again later, was seen by some senior managers within the company as valuable and impressive.

The main ways in which the philosophy was to be pursued however ensured it was to be primarily an inward looking exercise, concerning itself only with individual values and managerial styles. While the broader questions involved in the notion of 'stewardship' were certainly to interest some people, Hill presents no evidence of a 'main channel' by which progress to such goals was to be achieved. Since, in our study, we did not hear of one, we concluded that no such channel had existed.

This last point relates directly to our earlier analysis of the varying intentions of E.R.P. and the Tavistock people. The former felt that social science support was needed to draft a statement of philosophy so that employees attitudes might change and their behaviours would thus become more compatible with management's goals. The E.R.P. Unit can be characterised as 'a character in search of an author'. The Tavistock people with their vision of 'turbulent environments', and opinions of how large companies would find it necessary to change their conventional roles, saw a broader picture. They were 'authors in search of a character'. The confusing thing was, that the play the Tavistock authors wrote was not quite what the actors at Shell had in mind.

We do not wish to be misunderstood here. We are not saying that the company's top management cynically preached one thing while it practised something else. Our point is simply that their business frame of reference inevitably meant that efforts and resources were subsequently to be directed more in certain directions. The inward looking emphasis which characterised the company's efforts to implement the philosophy is quite unremarkable in this respect, although as we discuss later external developments (e.g. governmental wage policies) were to exert a considerable and for many an unexpected influence upon the fate of the philosophy exercise.

In this chapter we begin to describe what happened after the philosophy dissemination by considering first the demonstration job redesign projects and second the idea of dissemination via departmental managers. We consider also a very special case of such dissemination that has had wide publicity outside the company yet enjoys little acclaim today within it.

THE PILOT PROJECTS

We have already noted how E.R.P. were well aware that the philosophy conferences had raised people's expectations and that should nothing tangible emerge soon they were likely to come down with a bump. The pattern of reactions to the conferences that we reconstructed in the last chapter clearly showed how accurate this analysis was. The first way the possibilities of the philosophy were to be demonstrated was by the establishment by the Tavistock of a number of demonstration job redesign projects in the company. These were to demonstrate what 'joint optimisation' was all about, and would, it was hoped, encourage imitators.

That the Tavistock team hit upon the idea of a series of demonstration job redesign projects as a vehicle for meeting the need for progress, was no accident. At the very time they were working in Shell the Tavistock Institute was also involved in another pioneering venture in Norway. This project amounted to nothing less than an attempt to use social science ideas in the formulation and execution of a national policy concerning the involvement of people in industry. The strategies which evolved in this ambitious exercise, seemed very suitable for employment in the Shell project.

The early results of the Norwegian Industrial Democracy Project had been published in Norwegian in 1964 (1). This publication presented a closely argued case for thinking that the notion of industrial democracy should not be understood simply to refer to particular forms of the representation of workers in the process of a company's management. Later in the Project a series of carefully selected factories were chosen to be used as demonstration sites for what would be achieved in industrial democracy through the use of autonomous work groups. Naturally enough, the theoretical framework behind the belief in the value and feasibility of such a programme of industrial democracy was the idea of socio-technical systems analysis, (the same notions of 'joint optimisation' that had been presented to Shell). The Tavistock Institute did in fact provide much welcomed support to the Norwegians, the results of the work being reported originally in 1970 (2).

Since those days Norwegian social scientists involved in the demonstration projects have acknowledged that their initial hopes that autonomous groups would 'catch on' in Norway and be widely emulated there have very largely been disappointed (see, for example, Herbst, 1976). In the circumstances of the early 1960's it may be that the strategy they had adopted to encourage wide introduction of new ideas of industrial democracy, (i.e. demonstration projects) was the only feasible one at that time. Be that as it may, they did not appreciate the potential shortcomings of an approach where, in effect, social scientists set up new situations then stood around expectantly waiting for other people to copy them. And not appreciating the difficulties it was exactly this strategy that the Tavistock people adopted in Shell to back up the philosophy programme.

Looking back now at the demonstration projects that were set up in Shell it has to be said that they do creak a bit. As we shall see the methodology used in the first of them was ponderous and the demands of their administration were badly miscalculated. Yet it should not be forgotten that these were pioneering projects. As with other aspects of this whole project, for example the question of a business's social responsibilities, the Tavistock people were ahead of their time. It was only later that questions of 'the social responsibility of business' were to become a fashionable topic for discussion in industrial circles. It was only later also that social scientists were to find it fashionable to contribute to the job redesign literature. In 1966 people did not know what they know now about this area.

But having said this, and even acknowledging that a number of benefits did develop out of the projects in Shell (not the least of which was an attempt to de-mystify socio-technical systems analysis) certain firm conclusions have to be drawn: Shell's demonstration job redesign projects failed categorically to capture people's imaginations concerning the golden promises of 'joint optimisation'.

In June of 1966 at Stanlow, where as we have seen enthusiasm was greatest, three pilots were begun. Their success, at best, was patchy. One was abandoned within six months. A second proceeded well enough through the analysis of the technical stage, but after group interviews were held (which produced many suggestions for improvement) as part of the analysis of the social system, a period of extended delay took place. Finally, some small and beneficial changes were introduced in one small section of the department concerned.

More went on in connection with the third study. It took till February 1967 for a report to be submitted, and July 1967 for an action plan to be devised on it. Some action proposals were then found to overlap with the proposed areas of productivity bargaining and were abandoned. Others were dropped away. But a few (including the formulation of departmental objectives, and improved operator training and departmental communications) were used and felt to be useful by management.

Quite how useful this project had been was the subject of discussion between departmental and refinery management, and representatives of E.R.P. and the Tavistock in November of that year. The minutes of this meeting record that the general view was that the changes had been of some use, and were likely to improve the department's performance. Problems of evaluating some of the less tangible benefits (such as improved discussion between management and operators) were recognised. Some managers took the view that the changes were unremarkable, although the atmosphere generated by the philosophy exercise in general and this pilot project in particular had enabled them to materialise rather more smoothly and quickly than otherwise would have been the case.

Yet in terms of the wider operation the E.R.P./ Tavistock view was quite blunt and down-to-earth. The minutes of the meeting record:

'They believed, with the advantage of hind-sight, that some difficulties had perhaps been caused by the way the projects had been launched and developed, with for example a select group spending seven or eight months on the process of analysis before coming up with its report. This had helped the growth of expectations throughout the refinery of dramatic and fundamental changes in organisational structure or working methods; expectations that were clearly unwarranted.

Thus virtually any proposals or changes less
than revolutionary were almost from the outset, doomed to be received with a certain
amount of disappointment and to be coloured
with the tinge of failure'.

This evaluation is echoed in Trist's more general
comments (in Hill, (op.cit.), p.200):

'Three pilot projects were set up in one of
the large refineries but they did not go well.
They were too slow and open to disruption by
day to day pressures and from changes in key
personnel. Moreover, the degree of
concentration on these drained resources from'
other possibilities. This was resented.
The pilot projects were to some extent in
contradiction to the spirit of the whole
undertaking which had aimed to include
everyone'.

One of the people we spoke to at Stanlow expressed
a similar view. Recalling that the pilot projects had
been discussed at site management meetings which he
had attended, he felt:

'Generally, by the end, people didn't feel
too favourable towards them. People's
expectations had been raised too high. They
were unrealistic. Then there seemed to be
a lot of work involved and this came as a
shock. And the results weren't too tangible
either'.

The lessons were well learned. Efforts were already
in motion to produce a simplified method of socio-
technical analysis and another (called 'role analysis')
designed for use in administrative or service
departments.

The methods were introduced to interested parties,
and the simplified socio-technical analytic system
was employed on a fourth pilot project. This was

undertaken in a much shorter time period, (it was completed by the end of 1967) and in contrast to previous pilot projects, the plant manager here was involved immediately as proposals for change emerged, not this time being kept in suspense until the appearance of a written report.

Unfortunately, despite the now superior methodology used, this demonstration project, also laboured under disadvantages (3). The plant itself was a problem and it was already scheduled for replacement. Work in the plant (moulding bitumen into transportable blocks) was untypical of the bulk of jobs in the refinery, and the people engaged in the work ('it was awful, filthy and monotonous' we were told by someone then involved with its management) were not reckoned to be typical of the workers elsewhere employed in the refinery. Perceptions such as these made it easy for people to dismiss this project as less-than-relevant to their problems despite the fact that it was reasonably successful.

Two other points should be made here. A successful job redesign project initiated, interestingly enough by workers representatives (see Hill (op.cit.), p.157, did take place at Shell Haven. However this highly successful project was not initiated from any desire to demonstrate the principles of joint optimisation. It was a project, lasting six months, to see how practicable were ideas of work reorganisation that were being considered for the productivity bargains we discuss in the next chapter.

Also it is appropriate to record that, despite the failure of the Stanlow pilot studies to capture the enthusiasms that had been generated by the philosophy conferences, work in this area did not cease altogether. In 1967 and 1968 the Tavistocks' method of role analysis was tried with some success in two projects. In 1969 also, Herzberg-style methods were adopted in an attempt to enrich the jobs of supervisors in three departments, though here again continued diffusion of the projects did not subsequently take place.

The main point we are making in this section is a simple one. As a 'main channel' through which the philosophy was expected to realise its anticipated benefits, these demonstration projects were not successful.

DEPARTMENTAL MANAGERS AS CHANGE AGENTS

At the same time that the pilot studies were being undertaken dissemination of the philosophy was continuing. An essential part of the success of the total project was that the managers should discuss the philosophy with their staff and begin to manage their departments according to its principles.

In this section we describe what happened to this plan.

First we consider the early efforts made to disseminate the philosophy through departmental meetings, and to record early progress through an evaluation report. Then we explore the developing climate in which implementation of the philosophy was expected to be continued.

(i) Departmental philosophy conferences

At Stanlow four briefing sessions were held to help people plan how they would run their departmental discussions. This did not happen at Shell Haven, but here, of course, a proportion of shop floor level employees had attended the major dissemination conferences.

There is no way of knowing precisely how many such departmental meetings were held and in what manner (4). Informed sources, people who organised the other conferences, suggested their incidence and success was patchy. A comment from Shell Haven: 'We assumed supervisors would pass the message on. But we had

68

found the conferences hard to run you know, so it was
not surprising others did not pass it on'.

We did hear of the occasional success story. At
Stanlow in one department, discussion of the philosophy
flourished into a series of problem solving sessions
with section leaders. A list of twenty one action
points resulted, covering, in the main, 'questions of
responsibility and freedom'. The manager who
initiated these meetings thought they 'were neither
unique, nor common'.

Another manager, also from Stanlow, confirmed the
uneven pattern of continued dissemination. (He was
the self-styled 'missionary' from whom we quoted
earlier).

'The idea was that the manager should initiate
discussion for all employees about the
philosophy. It was bloody hard to do this.
It took a year and it was very hard to sell.
A lot of the people had left school at
fourteen, and I spent half the time
explaining words, what the philosophy meant.
There was a lot of cynicism around; all this
was within two or three years of the
demanning exercise. And the idea of
participative management was alien to some
people who thought they would loose their
power and authority.

I think now that you can't buy loyalty, you
have to earn it. We were trying to get people
interested in working for a profitable and
efficient company, like you have in America.
There was an element of brainwashing. You
can't change a management style on a whim,
a fad, a belief.

On the further dissemination some people
acted as missionaries, others had great
difficulty. I did a lot of reading to make

my own mind about it. Some of my colleagues
were saying it was rubbish. Others were
really wrapped up in it'.

(ii) The interim evaluation reports

Around this period, at the end of 1966, approximately
twelve months after top management had approved the
philosophy statement, while conferences were still
progressing at Shell Haven (they had finished at
Stanlow) and after the pilot projects had been
launched at Stanlow, top management requested a report
from each of the refineries on progress to date. In
April 1967 the reports were presented.

They are remarkable documents. Each includes an
estimate of costs involved, a report on how the
philosophy was launched, an assessment of progress,
and a long and detailed list of all the changes
departmental managers were able to report as
occurring since the start of the exercise. These
changes were reported in some detail, arranged under
the headings of 'Changes in organisation or
procedures', 'Redesign of jobs', 'Increased personal
commitment and responsibility' and 'More effective
pursuit of company objectives'.

The overall comments included in the reports are
revealing. In the Stanlow report it was noted that
appreciation of the philosophy was thinly spread over
a wide area and emphasised the continuing need to
improve people's understanding of it. The Shell Haven
report pointed to the amount of time the philosophy
exercise had taken up with no short term returns and
suggested 'too much may have been tackled too soon with
too limited resources'.

Despite these provisos Hill is probably correct when
he states that 'the overall impression created by the
results of the assessment review was, therefore, very
positive'. The copious list of changes reported at
Stanlow were practically all positive. At Shell Haven

some adverse changes were recorded but these were very much in the minority. Here also a positive series of changes was indicated.

So far as the effect of these documents on what happened subsequently is concerned it is this positive ambience that is the significant feature of them. No one would deny the reports give an impression of great activity. It is the reliability of this that some now question. A senior manager comments: 'It was a difficult exercise to do. People could not be pinned down'.

And a manager who was himself trying hard to implement the philosophy recalls:

> 'We had regular management meetings you
> know, looking for gains from the exercise.
> It seems unrealistic now to have looked for
> tangible results so quickly'.

The most outspoken critic of this episode, a man at Stanlow, said:

> 'Lots of little things happened after the
> conferences. There were postmortems,
> justifications, and a statement of how
> attitudes had changed after the meetings.
> It was all "in praise of".
>
> But I didn't like the document. There was
> one report which said provision had been
> made for building chimney stacks higher
> so there would be less pollution of the
> environment locally. This, it was claimed,
> was done to meet the objectives of the
> philosophy. My disenchantment ran wild at
> this. I didn't think it was true. I didn't
> think the philosophy had any effect on things
> like that. There were very good technical
> reasons for changing the design of the stacks.
> I think, really, that this sort of thing took

more from the credibility of the <u>people</u> concerned rather than the philosophy. And there were other examples ....

Then, you know, many people became dis-enchanted with the concepts. "You must consult" was the message. Well, there was a design change that affected my outfit. Normally I would have sat down with one or two and worked something out. But now I called everyone together to talk about it. Six months later we had got nowhere at all! They were arguing over every little tiny point .... So I just had to get out of it. "Argue if you like" I said. I went back to telling them.

We were being asked to believe that we are all a band of happy chaps moving towards a common goal. That is just not true.

And the aftermath of this, too, was a disaster. They used to come back at me: "I wanted to do this or that, but you wouldn't let me". So I had a band of delinquents on my hands now! With unlimited time it might have worked, but the investment of time and the degree of skill required was too high!

People don't kick against the accepted story. My experience of this failed experiment in participation was not reported in the evaluation report. There were very few reports of failures. You only heard about the ostensively good ones. The feeling of the times was "this is good"!'

As Trist acknowledges (in Hill op.cit., p.202) 'a wealth of qualitative material was obtained (in the reports) which served the immediate operational purpose' but they contained 'little that could be treated quantitatively'. It was suggested to us that

the technical culture within Shell made it necessary
to 'quantify' results in order to be able to adequately
defend the exercise. Hill (p.174) acknowledges the
former point but does feel able to add, 'taken together
(the changes that were logged) represent a clear and
positive movement towards the objectives embodied in
the philosophy statement'. As we have seen, not
everyone can agree with this opinion. Certainly, it
can hardly be claimed the methodology of the evaluation
studies was without its problems. It is easy to see
why the episode took on the appearance of a propaganda
exercise in soem people's minds, who thought that the
whole attempt to try to establish changes in this way
was itself just another example of the exuberance
that generally characterised the company philosophy
exercise.

Now, some ten years later, no one we spoke to took
the trouble specifically to itemise what changes had
taken place since that early and ambitious attempt to
document changes. It would be thought absurd if
people were now to be asked to do this in the style of
the. 1967 evaluation study. Beneficial changes were
to occur, as we discuss later, but the main threads
of the story at this stage lead elsewhere.

(iii) The developing climate of implementation

The main threads of this story lead to the conclusion
that this second main channel of implementation,
utilising departmental managers, was largely to dry up
just as the first one had done. The people who found
they had been placed in the front line of the
campaign were to find that the pressures on them to
continue the good work were soon to become both less
immediate and less credible.

The speed at which this happened varied at the
different refineries and in different areas within
each of them. At Stanlow the process is better
remembered today mainly, we suspect, because the
initial enthusiasm of the philosophy had been so much

73

more in evidence there, yet the processes at both Stanlow and Shell Haven were very similar.

The early results of the exhortations that managers should implement the philosophy have been implicit in our description of events so far:

(a)   The philosophy had been launched with a 'fanfare of trumpets'. The support of top management had carefully been wooed, although even here was <u>some</u> evidence of bulldozer tactics. Later certainly, the sell was to become rather harder.

(b)   Reactions to the philosophy were very varied, although people in favour seemed to be winning the day. Some did not understand it. Many saw it in the context of the period of austerity the company had just passed through.

(c)   Managers were encouraged to become more participative. For some this was not easy, nor successful. At both refineries also we were told of more management meetings now taking place. Some people regarded this as a short-lived trend towards 'management by committee'. All such attempts were doubtless well intended, though some misguided and others poorly done. The net outcome was a common feeling that early experiences in applying the philosophy were patchy in their success.

(d)   No social skills training or other back-up support of significance was provided. Exhortation, enthusiasm, perhaps a feeling that failures in all this tended not to have a respectable status – they were all people were given.

(e)   Many of the people involved in this process were technical men. For them the immense work load put upon them after the conferences seemed to be producing very slow results.

(f)   The pilot studies were disappointing and did not inspire confidence.

(g)   People thought there may be more in the philosophy for the weekly paid people (in terms of single status) than seemed to be true for the staff.   But it was difficult to get the weekly paids to understand this.

Very broadly the above developments summarise the story as we have so far told it.   Certainly the efforts that were made did produce some successes.   But this analysis suggests that they were only achieved after certain costs had been incurred.   How significant were these costs to be?

A most important aspect of the answer to this had to be provided by senior management.   Having initiated the exercise, what happened next would show how seriously they were taking it.

There were indeed some positive signs that stood out of all the talk.   Joint working parties were a novel development (see the next chapter), training staff had been appointed at more senior grades than ever before, and a 'Resources Manager' (see chapter seven) had been appointed at Shell Haven.

But some doubts remained.   The union representatives, as Hill reports, wanted firmer assurances about manning levels than could be supplied by the company. Managers, as he also notes, wondered how committed the Royal Dutch Shell group, (of which Shell Refining was but a part), would prove to be in their support.   We learnt also that it was not to pass unnoticed that the Board of Shell UK, while it had been informed of developments, was never formally to adopt the philosophy as 'official' (5).   Certain incongruities were reported at Shell Haven between the message of the philosophy and the style of manager B at the philosophy dissemination conferences themselves.

It was inevitable that managements' behaviours were
to be compared from now on with the principles they
had painted on the wall for others to follow. This
seems particularly to be true at Stanlow from where we
heard of the following developments.

At Stanlow criticisms were often made of managements'
proposals, sometimes in fun, sometimes rather more
cynically as part of bargaining tactics: 'you can't do
that, it's against the philosophy'. But there were
occasions, early on, when some people were to be
genuinely convinced that management had reneged on its
declared principles. An emotive example of this came
in 1967 when manager A who was enthusiastic about the
philosophy, had to face an overtime ban by his refinery
operators that was to last three months.

At this time there was one plant turning out
particularly good production figures, but in which
overtime had been cut, quite drastically, to the order
of 400% over that worked two years before. The (then)
manager noted that 'this was a lot of money out of a
lot of pockets', yet the men had continued to work very
hard. But one afternoon during the overtime ban
manager A 'phoned in to say that if a specified
quantity of products was not available by the next day
because the men refused to work overtime, they would be
laid off. The ex-plant manager told us:

> 'We'd had all this spirit on the unit, and a
> motto: like "the Windmill" we never closed ....
> but to hear what he said! And after all this
> philosophy of truth multiplied by kindness ....
> I thought he'd gone balmy!'

Later, things are reported to have continued to sour
during this ban.

> 'We really took a lot of stick then. What
> we did was to enforce things in the union
> agreements that we had never enforced before.
> The men said: "When your backs are to the wall,
> then where's your bloody philosophy?"'

It was about two years later with manager A's
successor that another incident we were told about
occurred. Genuinely, we are certain, a representation
on behalf of junior supervisory staff appealed to the
spirit of the philosophy in support of the point of
view they were expressing:

> 'What has happened to the philosophy?' we
> asked. The manager replied that it didn't mean
> what we'd understood it to mean. He said
> 'It does not mean that management is going to
> submit to whims. We are not a parental
> organisation!'

> 'And you know after that it was back to formal
> relations again, "Mr" this and "Mr" that. But
> it was without the respect of the old days.
> We were disillusioned.

> No one mentions the philosophy now. Yes, if
> you ask me, my personal view is that we were
> conned'.

Of course there are always two sides to stories such
as these. (As one of our interviewees said 'If you
bully a parson and he hits you back, it's a bit silly
to say "But ah! You're meant to be a man of God!"').
Management would have its own point of view on
incidents like these. But it is an indisputable fact
that they were not always thought to be acting
consistently just at the times when it really
mattered that they should. And, indeed, senior people
nowadays willingly admit that things went awry. 'We
did too much talking' was the comment. 'There was a
lack of imagination high up as to how to put the
philosophy into practice, what its implications were'.
This was hardly surprising, of course, in a project
where radical changes in the basic manner in which
a company managed its affairs were promised 'at a
stroke'.

While senior management was loosing the initiative in
the process of implementation, other counterproductive

77

(for the philosophy) developments were taking place.
Specifically, there was a very rapid movement of
managerial graded staff in and out of jobs in the
Shell UK refineries. A survey carried out around now
showed that, on average, people only held such jobs
for around eighteen months. There was a lot of coming
and going.

We understand from discussions with an ex-member of
E.R.P., that the E.R.P. had hoped that as the
philosophy had taken hold in the company, people would
not move from other companies in the Royal Dutch Shell
group into Shell refining unless they were prepared to
manage according to its principles. It was indeed
confidently expected that this policy would be
implemented. In fact, attitudes to the philosophy
seem to have played no part at all in the selection
process for jobs in Shell refining. People were to
move into key posts who had neither attended philosophy
conferences nor had the slightest intention to manage
their affairs by reference to the philosophy statement.
This seemed particularly noticeable at Stanlow. As
one of our interviewees put it: 'the needs of Shell
group for international commitments was not compatible
with the time span needed to consolidate the
philosophy'.

This becoming evident, career minded people were to
see the philosophy was substantially irrelevant to
their general career prospects in the Royal Dutch Shell
group. What did matter for this was a good technical
record. In junior and middle management positions
that were filled on a more local basis it probably is
true that henceforth questions of man-management skills
were taken more into account, but such considerations
seemed of little relevance regarding international
movements.

Movement at refinery manager level itself was also
proceeding apace in the post 1965 period. Manager B
had left Shell Haven in 1969. His second successor
nine months later was perceived by some as

unsympathetic towards the philosophy. Manager A had
left Stanlow in 1967. His immediate successor
apparently showed little more interest in the
philosophy, and he was supported in this by the views
of the new personnel manager. In 1970 the top job at
Stanlow changed hands again, going this time to
Manager B. His style and actions now, despite the
fact of his original involvement in the exercise, left
people at Stanlow well aware that 'the philosophy' no
longer cut much ice with him.

At a higher level still in the company it is widely
believed now that the managing director who had
originally launched the project only retained an
active personal interest in it for about eighteen
months. Subsequently no one reported to us any
visible and positive support emanating from that level.

We can therefore sum up these points and continue
our analysis of the ailing policy that departmental
managers should be the 'main channel' for the
philosophy implementation:

(h) It seemed that certain 'costs' were being
     incurred in people's efforts to implement
     the philosophy. To assess how worthwhile
     they were people tended to look toward the
     behaviour of their superiors.

(i) Important inconsistencies were seen. Top
     management lost the initiative in the matter.

(j) Rapid staff movements were taking place at
     this time. Commitment to the philosophy was
     not considered a relevant factor when
     appointments were made at senior levels in
     Shell Refining.

(k) For people interested in their international
     careers in the Royal Dutch Shell group, as
     ever what mattered was a good technical record.
     The investment of time and effort required

in becoming known as a good manager of men
seemed distracting and irrelevant.

(1)   By 1970 the refinery managers at Shell Haven
       and at Stanlow were both known as not being
       very sympathetic towards 'the philosophy'.
       There was no visible or tangible support for
       it from higher levels. Some other key posts
       within the refineries were also to be filled
       by people not committed, or even known to be
       opposed, to the philosophy.

   Here, then, was hardly an appropriate atmosphere for
departmental managers to take risks and attempt major
changes of policy. We do not say all was completely
lost. We are simply illustrating how unrealistic it
was, in this developing environment, to expect departmental heads to act as a leading edge of the type of
organisation changes that architects of the philosophy
had in mind.

   Before turning to discuss the remaining 'main
channels' of the philosophy's intended implementation,
we now discuss events at Stanlow's wax plant.

THE WAX PLANT EPISODE

Between 1966 and 1969 an attempt was made to introduce
participation into the daily management of affairs at
the wax department at Stanlow. The episode is
mentioned by Hill (op.cit., p.121) as 'a good example
of how the better utilisation of operators'
capabilities could improve performance'. Changes
introduced here in both the social and technical
systems meant that 'the performance of the department
and the morale of the employees improved significantly'.

   Changes at the wax plant in fact were not introduced
with the help of E.R.P. and Tavistock people although
the changes were assisted and encouraged by the
philosophy. The developments at the wax plant were not
given the status of a 'Pilot Project' but were the

result of the (then) plant manager's enthusiastic efforts to begin himself to introduce new approaches to management.

Our interest in the wax plant story was aroused for a number of reasons. Here was an example of a spontaneous and self directed introduction of new practices very much, it seemed, in the spirit of the philosophy exercise. Moreover, it was widely known about in the company, more widely perhaps than are the 'official' philosophy demonstration projects. In the minds of some people, the wax plant episode was a good example of what the philosophy was all about.

Second, correctly or incorrectly, reports of developments at the plant were criticised by some of the people we spoke to, sometimes very severely. Their depth of feeling was itself data for us in our study of what had happened to the philosophy and we wanted to look further into the episode.

There was also a third reason why we decided to attempt to pick up the threads of this story. This is because of the publicity it has been given outside the refinery. While the wax plant story is not now much respected in the company, a number of favourable reports have been published for various outside interest groups; for scholars and anyone interested in the close study of 'the quality of working life' (6), for managers generally (Taylor, 1972a), and for people in the oil industry itself (Taylor, 1972b). When we came across the wax plant episode, we were already feeling that Shell's company philosophy seemed to be held in more respect by people outside the company than by people within it; perhaps the same was true of the wax plant story?

In presenting this story we rely on two sources of information. The first is provided by the published reports of developments at the wax plant by Burden (1975) the manager of the plant between 1966 and 1969, and by Taylor (1972a and 1972b) who was not involved herself in the episode. (These accounts vary slightly,

in the amount of detail they include, but it is evident
that the Taylor reports are, almost word for word,
based on the Burden accounts).

Six people working in Shell provided our second
source of information. Four were people with
detailed knowledge of the wax plant's operations
during and around the crucial 1966-69 period. The
other two were people who had been closely associated
with its management subsequent to this period.

First for some background. The wax plant opened
in 1962 as a unique plant, one of less than a handful
of such intricate and advanced wax generating plants
in the world. At its opening some of the best
operators at Stanlow were appointed to work in it.
Indeed, the work was (and remains) attractive to
process operators; there are several processes
involved in the plant so the work is varied and offers
good experience for promotion. The operators themselves are required to carry out more observation of
equipment than is usual for the site as a whole and it
is also easier to identify with an end product in this
plant than is the case in many continuous flow process
plants. Characteristically, we were told, there was
a good spirit in the plant. Also characteristic of
it were certain operating problems; it was a difficult
plant to run.

The Burden report discusses how in 1966 the new wax
plant manager found that he faced a difficult short
term crisis. A type of feedstuff different from the
one the plant had been designed to use was having to
be fed into it, serious problems were developing as a
result with perhaps a total plant shutdown threatened.
Unfamiliar himself with the difficult wax technology
of the plant the new manager turned to his senior staff
for counsel.

Apparently this was an ususual development in this
department. Because of the difficult state of the
plant the previous manager had forbidden the operators
to allow modifications to its operating condition

unless he himself first gave the word. It is reported
that this style of management had breeded resentment
amongst the operators who consequently had tended not
to speak up with ideas for overcoming problems.

   However, the new plant manager's meeting with his
senior staff was a success and with their help somehow
the very pressing short term, operating problems were
overcome.

   The new manager, indeed, decided his basic task was
to 'develop a will to win' amongst his staff (see
Burden op.cit., p.204, Taylor 1972a, p.54 and 1972b,
p.141). Thereafter a regular weekly meeting with them
became a feature of his management. Operators, as well
as management staff, were included and the meetings
were subsequently always held in the operators' mess
room. The climate of the company, following the
company philosophy exercise, encouraged such
innovations of course.

   Partly as a result of ideas the staff put up
themselves in these meetings and partly as a result of
the comments they made on the manager's suggestions,
over the 1966-69 period a number of changes were made
in the plant. The Burden and Taylor reports present
an impressive list of them. What they amount to are
claims for the introduction of a different system of
organisation in the plant with

(a)   operators becoming much more autonomous within
      each shift on how the plant should be run (7),
      and

(b)   junior managerial staff accepting some of the
      functions previously undertaken by the plant
      manager (8).

   In describing these modifications the Burden and
Taylor reports adopt an enthusiastic tone. The message
they deliver is that this is an exciting success story
that deserves to be emulated. Taylor (1972a, p.64 and
1972b, p.144) says the company

'found out that men are capable of doing more,
much more, and not necessarily with a price
tag'.

Burden (op.cit., p.213) amplifies:

'It is suggested .... that there is a considerable
latent talent in industry waiting to be used if
only the opportunity is given. Men are capable
generally of doing more, much more, than
managements currently allow them to do and if
only 10% of this latent talent were released
we might see a considerable change in national
economic fortunes'.

Some data is offered in support of the success of the
new arrangements. Regarding absenteeism, Burden offers
statistics suggesting percent days lost was lower in
the wax plant than in the refinery as a whole, though
rising by 1969. Regarding promotions, he makes much
play of the high numbers of operators promoted to
more senior jobs outside the plant. He attributes
this to the wide experience people obtained in the now
more flexible wax plant operating system (9).

Regarding the plant's productivity, Burden reports
that following some suggestions of the staff
significant technical improvements were made.
Importantly as well he claims a 100% increase in output was achieved in one section of the plant because
of the increased motivation of workers over this
period:

'This part of the plant was extremely demanding
because its sixteen operating variables had to
be closely controlled .... This is the type of
job which can successfully be accomplished only
by highly motivated operators, and the output
increase indicated is a measure of the success
achieved .... The whole unit appeared to be
under (the operators) control, and this was
exactly the objective'. (Burden op.cit., p.213.

Emphasis added. See also Taylor 1972a, p.61 and 1972b, p.144).

This, then, is a success story indeed. Bringing it up to date in 1972 (Taylor says, 'This, then, is the present ....') we are told that following Stanlow's productivity deal craftsmen were more easily integrated to the operating teams on the wax plant than was true elsewhere. And Burden (in the paper he read at a 1972 conference but which was not published for another three years) says:

'It is over three years now since the author left the plant and in that time the new departmental manager has carried on, extending the style of management adopted in 1966 ....

The present manager has increased still further the responsibility of the departmental supervisors to the point where they are now virtually running the department'. (Burden op.cit., p.214).

But meanwhile, back at the plant, sad to tell, all was by no means well. In 1972 in fact, the wax plant manager (the second since Burden's departure) was having 'fantastic trouble' with the plant. He was to leave in 1972 having been unable to stem a seemingly irreversible and calamitous downward trend in the plant's productivity. The new manager and the task force he arrived with, charged with the task of putting things to right, were then to act under the harsh beam of a spotlight trained on the affair by no less a person than the manufacturing director of Shell UK himself.

The fact, then, that people in the company now dismissed the newly published Taylor reports with a few well chosen words will come as no surprise.

What had happened in the wax plant? An operator of the 1966-69 period recalled the style of the manager of that time:

'He was a reasonable man, with a good approach.
I liked him, he treated you as a person.
People recognised he was different, participative.
Meanwhile, experience of the plant had been
building up, it could be used. Technically
he was no better than others but his approach
was good.

He wanted the men to get involved, and achieved
this through group meetings. We used to discuss
what we felt about operating faults at them.
It made you feel part of the job. He was
successful in this. He generated enthusiasm ....'

Other (then) operators paid tribute to how the plant
meetings of the 1966-69 era had helped communications
and efficiency. Quite how far reaching the associated
organisational changes were, was a point of some
debate: one person we spoke to said he had not himself
liked the (as he described it) 'Hail fellow, well met!'
approach, and felt himself there was more talk than
action at this time. Be that as it may, others did
praise the good sense of changes introduced in this
period. The abolition of clocking, for example, was
considered particularly sensible (10).

At this time also it is true to say that the
operators did achieve the occasional very good day.
Production records set now were to stand for some time.
The plant was making money. Yet all was not right.
The quality of the wax produced in what seemed such
large quantities was reportedly 'atrocious'. So much
so that we were told the records were to become to
be regarded as less of a shining example and more of
a standing joke.

The instability of the plant was to become evident
in other ways also. After acknowledging that the
occasionally very good day was achieved in this period
a member of the task force who was later to help sort
out the developing mess said that, nonetheless, the
plant's capacity was not fully being tested at this

time. 'No one was asked to "open the tap". When we did, nothing came out'.

Quite why this was to happen no one at the time understood. But happen it did. Indeed the production of on-grade wax began to go into steep decline. Nowadays people recall that this began around 1968/69. The precise time that performance was identified as deteriorating seems somewhat immaterial however, for quite soon the position was to become desperate. Several hundred thousand pounds had been put into the plant in an effort to improve matters but apparently to no avail. The matter was now so serious that it had begun to attract critical comment from top management in London.

A task force was set up to investigate the wax plant. Urgent high level meetings were regularly held to monitor progress. The plant manager was replaced.

Progress did not come quickly. As if to compound other difficulties the plant's senior supervisor and his foreman were to retire due to ill health within a few days of each other. The new manager himself was placed under a lot of pressure and was now unable to call upon the two experienced supervisors who had had to retire. The plant's operators initially (though not later) were frightened of him, 'one mistake and he'll sack me' they thought.

Of the many contributory causes that were to be identified as behind the crisis, two emerged as crucial. The first was an urgent need to standardise the operating conditions of the plant. A series of 'bad habits' had crept in. So much was this the case that in terms of the instructions specified by the plant's designers on occasions the operators simply did not know what to do i.e. they were going the wrong things. As one person put it, a 'folk law' had built up as to how this very difficult plant was to operate. Moreover, as if to confound the situation each shift had developed its own separate folk law. Each tended to have its own way of doing things.

With the time lag involved when operating conditions were modified on the plant, the net result of this was that the plant was in a constant state of flux.

A second underlying factor was the need for greater precision concerning plant maintenance requirements. The tolerance levels of the machinery had in some respects been greatly over estimated and the importance of other details not understood.

It would be beyond our brief and capabilities to arbitrate on what was responsible for the developments at the wax plant. Apart from the complexity of the technology (which we do not understand) there is the difficulty anyway of apportioning blame for actions undertaken in the best of faith which only after a period of inertia may have led to unintended consequences. Indeed if one considers the range of factors which can potentially contribute to the level of productivity of this plant it is clear that the system of management is but one of a number. The knowledge and skill of the operating staff, the quality of feedstuffs, the quality of the plant, market demand and general efficiency of administration are all relevant. There was indeed some disagreement amongst our respondents as to the causes and timing of the decline in performance in the wax plant.

For the purpose of this report however it seems irrelevant to some extent whether or not production began to decline in 1968/69 or began later. It also seems largely irrelevant whether or not people are correct when they say that operators began to forget the fundamental things they should do at this time, or began later. What is more relevant here is a consideration of the steps that were taken at a later date to put these affairs to right. In several important respects improvement at this plant began from a re-organisation of the working system away from the system Burden and Taylor describe so enthusiastically. Especially, insufficient controls to ensure correct working in general and consistency across shifts in particular had been built into the system. And the rapid turnover of experienced operators from the plant, far from being accommodated in a system of flexible plant operators seems, in the event, to have facilitated the emergence of 'operating folklaws'. Perpetuated as they were and aggravated by inadequate maintenance it appears that these failings had a lot to do with the distressing events that were later to take place.

We have also to report that people within Shell were incensed at the appearance of rosy reports of an allegedly successful project apparently still moving from strength to strength. When things were badly wrong at the wax plant some people thought 'it was the "be nice" philosophy coming unstuck'. For them, publication by Taylor in 1972 of such positive reports seemed quite extraordinary, even irresponsible.

Nowadays knowledge about the plant's operation has been put to good use. We were told that twice as much as wax is now (1977) being produced with prospects also for additional significant improvements. In part these improvements are due to the utilisation of ideas of participation, although now also with a recognition that operators are not all equally capable and competent. Energy loss and chemical wastage too are greatly improved. From the point of view of the wax plant the story has a happy ending.

From the point of view of the philosophy exercise, however, the story does not end happily. The importance of the wax plant episode as an admittedly unintentioned piece of anti-philosophy propaganda should not be overlooked. In some people's minds today (see, for example, the quotation on p.123) the wax plant changes were the biggest experiment of the whole philosophy exercise. For many people the discovery that outside Shell these changes were presented as highly successful just at the time when things appeared to be going badly wrong led to a disillusionment with both the philosophy in particular and with applied social science in general.

NOTES

(1)   They were published in English some five years
later: see

Emery and Thorsrud (1969).

Fred Emery was an important member of the
Tavistock group working with Shell. Initially
this group was led by Eric Trist, but with his
departure in 1966, Emery took over this role
until his own departure a year later.

(2)   They were published in English some six years
later: see

Thorsrud and Emery (1976).

(3)   These were, almost certainly, understood at the
time. Hill reports (p.126) the reason this
project was chosen was the need to get quick
results (some preliminary work had been done on
this plant during the preparation of the
simplified analysis methods) coupled with a
'drastic shortage' of support staff at this time,
either from E.R.P. or the Stanlow personnel
department.

(4)   Stanlow reported to top management in April 1967
that all hourly paid staff had an opportunity to
attend a meeting but does not elaborate. Shell
Haven reported at the same time that a minority
of people did not wish to attend though most had
done so. At this date, the latest record we
knew of, eleven out of twenty-six departments
there had not held meetings. We presume it was
intended they would later but do not know how
many did so.

(5)   When the philosophy programme was initially
launched in the refineries they were organised
within a company named Shell Refining Company
Ltd. As noted above the Managing Director and

his senior staff supported and approved the launching of the exercise. In 1967 however Shell Refining was reorganised as part of a broader company, Shell UK Ltd. It was suggested to us that one reason the new board never officially and formally declared its support for the philosophy was that it regarded the exercise as a local matter, suitable for its refineries, that it had inherited from the old Shell Refining Ltd.

(6)   See Burden (1975). Originally this had been delivered as a paper at the 1972 International Conference on the Quality of Working Life.

(7)   Some of the reported changes included, for operators:

workloads modified to include more meaningful sections of the total process

increased flexibility within operating shifts

increased flexibility between shifts, with clocking being abolished and senior operators being made responsible for recording absenteeism and arranging cross shift cover

senior operators being allowed to modify plant operating conditions themselves

operators given authority over product quality control checks

operators being more involved in specifying maintenance requirements.

(8)   Changes for the senior supervisor and his foreman included:

producing plans for improved plant design

ordering major items of new equipment

drafting budget requirements and allocating
budget funds

selecting new operators.

(9)   Burden does acknowledge (p.212) that the rapid
        turnover of operators potentially caused problems
        for continued smooth running of the plant. Yet
        he claims their movement out of the place itself
        only reinforced the needs to develop flexibility
        of the operators on different functions within
        each shift. This then, he said, served to give
        these people the kind of experience likely to
        equip them for promotion in their turn.
        Accordingly a self perpetuating system emerged
        he says, to the satisfaction of all concerned.

(10)   It is correct to note however that according
        to the Stanlow 1967 evaluation report, by March
        1967 clocking had been abolished for no less
        than 2,100 out of the 2,900 employees previously
        affected by it. By no means, then, was this
        particular achievement at the wax plant a unique
        one.

6 Productivity Deals and the New Refinery

In accordance with the theme of our study we have been tracing the path of the philosophy from its beginnings in the E.R.P. report to top management of January 1965. It will be recalled, however, that in this report the E.R.P. Unit had envisaged a two pronged attack on the company's man-management problems of which the philosophy was but one part.

The philosophy programme had been the recommended vehicle for changing the company's management style in an attempt to improve employee attitudes towards their work and the company. It had also been recommended that revised agreements should be struck with the employees unions to end excessive job demarcations and to introduce staff status for weekly paid employees.

It had been intended that the two prongs of this operation would interlink. The philosophy was to prepare the way for the revised union agreements. The productivity bargains were to make it easier to continue implementing the principles of the philosophy. Hill's summary of this intended interaction of the E.R.P. Unit's twin proposals is shown on Figure 6.1. As the company was to brief its supervisors when the revised union agreements were introduced:

'The introduction of joint productivity planning (i.e. the new union agreements) did not spring directly from the philosophy conferences but it did spring from the same beliefs that gave rise to the philosophy document. The belief was that our human resources were not being effectively utilised ....' (Hill, op.cit., p.161)

Figure 6.1
'Schematic plan of ideal interaction of action proposals in solving the
problem at shop floor level'. From Hill (1971), p.147.

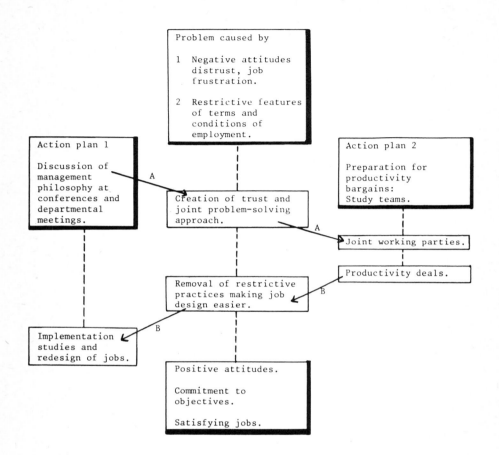

The reason why the revised union agreements were expected to support the philosophy programme relate to their radicality. Nothing less than staff status for hourly paid employees was being proposed. Annual salaries were to be paid instead of hourly rates. There were to be no payments for overtime. Increased flexibility between job functions were intended to reduce demarcations between jobs. Such changes as these, the E.R.P. Unit proposed, would fundamentally modify the relationship of shop floor employees and the company.

Some four or five years later revisions in the terms and conditions of weekly paid staff of this magnitude became operational. People now received a fixed annual salary being granted 'time-off-in-lieu' for any overtime worked but not being paid at premium rates for such work. Some flexibility between craftsmen's work was achieved and plant operators were now granted the rights to undertake minor maintenance work previously only undertaken by craftsmen. At Stanlow craftsmen were integrated into teams of operators, themselves assuming some operating functions. A system of 'group working' was introduced giving the men a measure of autonomy in arranging cover for absence amongst themselves.

In his account of the introduction of these agreements Hill basically emphasises three points. These are as follows:

(1) The philosophy exercise contributed very significantly to the successful introduction of the productivity bargains.

We have marked this link as path 'A' on Figure 6.1. Commenting on such a link Hill observes (p.167):

'To what extend the success achieved depended on the effects of the philosophy dissemination programme it is not possible to measure exactly. Certainly it was the opinion of the managements concerned that one could not have been achieved

95

without the other'.

Indeed Hill goes as far as to state (p.149) that the successful conclusion of productivity bargains was itself seen 'as an important criterion of success for the whole philosophy programme'.

(2)   Hill suggests that the process by which the productivity bargains were formulated should be considered more significant even than the structure of the agreements themselves.

We discuss strategies the company used to introduce the productivity deals below. There is no doubt that the company did experiment in its methods for formulating the bargains. The particular innovation that Hill commends so firmly in this process was the setting up of joint working parties of management and worker representatives. Together these two groups were to consider ways in which shop floor efficiency might be improved and the terms and conditions for shop floor level employees made more appropriate. These were not negotiating groups, bargaining over what price should be put on any acceptable proposals the working parties might propose was to take place later, but were joint problem solving groups. Hill refers to them as a 'main channel' by which the philosophy could be implemented.

Trist says (in Hill (op.cit.), p.201) these working parties constituted 'a major innovation in the conduct of industrial relations'. Hill himself says:

> 'More important than the content of the bargains
> – significant as that also was – was the manner
> in which they were arrived at. Both management
> representatives and union representatives were
> dedicated to the bargainings success and shared
> to a greater extent than ever before the same
> frame of reference'. (p.189)

(3)   Hill (in writing in 1971) indicates his belief
      that the prospects for continuing movement
      towards positive attitudes etc., as a result of
      the twin proposals of the philosophy and
      productivity deals, were good.

This is the path 'B' we have marked on Figure 6.1,
which illustrates the mutually supportive structures
and processes that Hill's unit wished to create. He
emphasises (p.160) the lengths to which the company
went to ensure the new structures of the productivity
deals would stand the test of time (1). And later,
even after acknowledging that there were some early
setbacks to the philosophy (see Hill's comments on
pp.183-5 of his book), he is able to conclude:

> 'Whether, therefore, the values and concepts
> of the philosophy statement are now sufficiently
> well embodied in the organisation to withstand
> any future setbacks, it is still too early to
> judge. The indications are that they are, but
> the next five years will show'. (p.186)

Our enquiry (conducted some six years after Hill was
writing) enabled us to review Hill's hopes and assess-
ments. In some respects they were supported. But in
others we found that events had moved in directions
diametrically opposed to those he had envisaged.
Following our discussion of the implementation of the
productivity deals we turn finally in this chapter to
a fourth 'main channel' of implementation; the
incorporation of the principles of the philosophy into
the design of a new refinery.

EVENTS LEADING TO THE SIGNING OF THE BARGAINS

The events that led to the signing of the productivity
bargains can be summarily outlined as falling into
four stages.

(a) Following the 1965 E.R.P. report management study
     teams collect data of the implications of the
     changes in the union agreements that had been
     proposed.

(b) In the second half of 1966 joint working parties
     (JWPs) of management and union representatives
     meet to consider ways of improving efficiency
     and the terms of employment for shop floor people.

     The constitution of these groups was new. They
     were not negotiating groups but problem solving
     groups. Previously Shell's management and worker
     representatives had not come together in such a
     way. Hill refers to these groups as a 'main
     channel' by which the company philosophy was to be
     realised.

(c) Later, in 1967, the JWPs were to be abandoned due
     to their slow (though not inconsiderable)
     progress (2). Early in 1968 management convened
     a second series of meetings with union
     representatives to agree, prior to negotiation,
     on the form and content of proposals for
     productivity deals.

     The important difference between these meetings
     and the earlier ones was that by now management
     had clear and preconceived ideas as to what it
     wanted. As an ex-member of the E.R.P. group put
     it to us: 'although it was not admitted at the
     time the industrial relations people had firm
     ideas the second time around'.

(d) Negotiations took place, beginning in 1968, and
     their outcomes were put to a ballot of union
     members for ratification. Eventually, though not
     always on the first ballot or by a particularly
     wide margin, the proposals were ratified. (This'
     happened in January 1969 for craftsmen at Stanlow,
     and in September for operators there. At Shell
     Haven the operators ratified their deal in
     October 1969. The craftsmen at this refinery,

who had not earlier participated in the joint working party scheme, agreed their deal only in November 1970).

Hill's account of these events concentrates on stages (a) and (b) above. He says very little about stages (c) and (d). Indeed, as we have already noted, in describing the role of the JWPs as a major channel by which the philosophy might be implemented, Hill's presentation emphasises a positive assessment of their significance in the story of the deals' successful introduction.

From our study we certainly have no doubt but that the shift from an exclusively bargaining relationship between management and unions in the refineries to one which allowed for some degree of collaboration was a major development. In terms of the history of troubled industrial relations that we outlined in an earlier chapter this was a significant departure from past practice.

Such as assessment was overwhelmingly endorsed by the people we spoke to during our enquiry. What they told us was that the changed spirit of the times, due very largely to the hopes and expectations created by the philosophy programme, was a major asset in securing the successful conclusion of the productivity deals. So much was this the case that we found the company philosophy and productivity deals had become blurred together in some peoples' minds. 'The productivity deals were seen as the manifestation of the philosophy' said one person we spoke to. 'There could have been no productivity deal without the philosophy' another thought.

For the great majority of our respondents the productivity deal and the philosophy were inextricably entwined. But we should note the existence of a small number of senior managers who either consistently maintained that they should be seen as separate factors or who claimed that once the two become confounded together for whatever reasons, the true spirit of the philosophy would be lost.

It is also necessary to record that there were other aspects to the launching of the productivity deals that raised difficulties. We heard of three that appear to be particularly significant.

First, (as Hill acknowledges) <u>it was the case that not everyone participating in the JWP programme was fully satisfied about the wisdom of this course of action.</u> The craftsmens' representatives at Shell Haven, for example, had taken the view that the company was simply looking for ways to overcome demarcation without saying what it was prepared to offer in return. Faced with this question-mark on its preparedness to adopt a genuinely participative approach to the company's management, top management at the refinery after some debate had disbanded this joint working party. But even elsewhere, while the process of joint working certainly did encourage the hopes of those who sought staff status for themselves and their colleagues, not everyone was convinced. A craft steward at Stanlow said to us:

'We were educating the company for nothing'.

When asked why they continued to do this he said:

'When the working parties were reinstated for the second time we had to go along because the company said "if you participate we may be able to make you an offer"'.

While some people certainly were impressed by management's desires to consult, and some were perhaps proud to be associated with a move radically to change shop floor employees terms and conditions of employment, the motivations of others who participated were more commonplace. Their involvement was, simply, instrumental.

The second difficulty with the proposal that collaborative relationships facilitated the movement towards the productivity deals comes from <u>accounts we heard of how final progress was made towards the formulation of the revised union agreements</u>. There is no doubt but that, originally, the JWPs conducted their affairs in more of a spirit of shared problem solving than ever before. Yet the novelty of this should not be allowed to obscure the point that initially these working parties should at best be more correctly described as consultative rather than collaborative. In his M.Sc. thesis Hibbert quotes from a comment on the JWPs at this stage made by the Industrial Relations Manager at Stanlow in a management forum held in 1969. The manager says:

'It is as well to remind you that at this stage the company had not fed in the concepts it had in mind, in other words we went into bat with the working parties with the blank piece of paper approach, except that the management representatives declared what they felt were impediments to efficiency e.g. restrictive practices, overtime. In hindsight we feel it would have speeded up the discussion had we exposed the concepts we had in mind at the outset and used the working parties to ferret out other concepts and to graft flesh onto bones. However, you will recall at this time the wage freeze was imposed upon us and perhaps this gave us a false impression that we had all the time in the world to allow participation/involvement to take its natural course.

For the first few months of the meetings which took place once a week (half day), most of the ideas being generated came from the management representatives, some of whom, you will recall, were present on all working parties. Obviously they were gently feeding in the concepts of the embryo plan and ensuring that cross fertilization between the JWPs was taking place'.

It has to be said that to describe this process as the introduction of collaborative management is mis- placed. Yet despite the unquestionably manipulative element of the process it was at this stage over- shadowed by the unprecedented extent to which management had chosen to discuss, explain and justify its ideas.

Yet the management's disenchantment with the JWPs was growing in 1967. Matters which required simultaneous progress on both the craft and operators joint working parties were not progressing, and action seemed very distant still. Also the unions had shown they were prepared to withdraw co-operation from the JWPs in protest over disputes elsewhere, whilst some union members were critical of their shop stewards on the JWPs for being too removed from shop floor realities. Management set to work therefore to decide itself precisely what it wanted. By August 1967 it was considered appropriate to reveal these to the union. A manager involved at this time said the following about what happened at this stage:

> 'From about 1968 management took the initiative. We went along to the meetings with blank sheets of paper, just like before. Our minds too had to appear to be blank! But it was really a process of re-education we were in from now on. Management knew what they wanted by now, but we had to lead the men.
>
> Change had to emanate from the same union as the men belonged to. A number of items appeared on the agenda, but we presented ideas as if they were off the top of our heads.
>
> Really, the second set of working parties was just a gimmick. They were just a way of moving towards the productivity deals'.

The comments of a union representative about this period provides a clue as to how this apparent spontaneity was engineered. While he fully understood

102

that the philosophy had been launched in 1966 this
interviewee nevertheless maintained that as a real
influence it did not emerge until after an industrial
dispute in mid 1967. 'After that', he said, 'it led
to the productivity deal'. Comments such as these,
taken with the close links people saw between the
philosophy and the productivity deals, tend to suggest
that references to the 'spirit of the philosophy'
were regularly being made around now as part of a
management campaign to formulate and implement the
revised union agreements it desired. A manipulative
element was predominant in management's dealings with
the unions at this time.

The third point we heard about, to moderate the claim
that improved collaborative spirit led to the
acceptance of the productivity deals, concerned the
nature of the cash bargain finally struck. Hill does,
of course, carefully point out that a distinction has
to be drawn between the work of the JWPs and the
subsequent bargaining over what price should be put on
whatever proposals they produced. Such distinction is
sensibly drawn. But it should not be understood to
mean that at the bargaining stage 'no holds are
barred'. Trist (p.201) makes a similar point when he
complements the way the JWPs had infused a committed
spirit to union and management representatives
involved in them. He says:

> 'The extent of (the JWPs) contribution was not
> recognised until the bargaining process itself
> got under way. They formed a new type of
> 'temporary system' and they exercised far-
> reaching influence as a 'reference group' even
> when they were no longer meeting'.

What is widely believed nowadays, however, is that
despite all the talk of collaboration and participation,
and despite the apparently new recognition of the
status of shop floor workers, when management came to
talk about money everything was 'up for grabs'.
Management drove a hard bargain over the productivity
deals. Managers and union people alike told us the

company was tight over the money it was prepared to
pay to end strict demarcations.

In 1966 Harold Wilson's government had introduced
the first of the many pay freezes in the UK. Wage
rises unaccompanied by increases in productivity were
to be forbidden. Rises had been agreed within Shell
just prior to the freeze (they included a small payment for the union's participation in the JWP scheme).
But other rises were to be held back till the
productivity deals were signed some three years later.
Understandably by then, as a shop steward involved in
the negotiations recalled:

> 'People felt they were on a cleft stick.
> Although there were some surprises in the
> proposals that we did not like - particularly
> an element of mandatory overtime was built
> into the deal - many people felt they had to
> accept what the company offered. We had been
> waiting so long for our money you see!'

A senior manager expressed a similar view:

> 'Shell got something for nothing. We had
> professional negotiators and their professional
> pride made them feel they had done something
> good. But it wasn't so! You don't win that
> way in a capital intensive industry!
>
> Some people say Shell wouldn't have put up
> the basic rate they were offering, for any
> reason. I just don't believe this'.

Of course some people did like the money the company
offered. But this offer was significantly lower than
that which the unions had claimed. And negotiations
were to carry on for many months. There was talk of
strike action on at least one occasion. At Stanlow
indeed, welders did not want to sign the craftsmens'
deal and stayed outside of it for a number of months
before they relented. There was opposition to the
deal, and the reasons for its acceptance do not easily

104

lend themselves to oversimplifications. One
commentator told us:

> 'when it came to the vote to accept or not
> to accept there were still many "antis".
> Although some of the men liked the money,
> some didn't really know, and many had been
> against originally. Others said "yes"
> without really understanding all the "ins
> and outs" of the deal'.

Returning to the three major points Hill makes about
the productivity bargains we are now in a position to
pass comment on the first two.

Firstly, it does seem correct to say that the
philosophy exercise did contribute to the successful
introduction of the productivity bargains. The joint
working parties were novel. The company philosophy
did promise a more dignified future for some people.

Yet our enquiries suggest it would be naive to
ignore the presence and importance of other factors.
The new mood of 'trust' and 'joint problem solving',
unusual and significant as it was, was not the whole
story. As we have seen factors that were also
important included:

(a) The perceptions by some of the people who
     participated in the joint working parties was that
     this was simply the best available method they had
     to obtain an offer of improved earnings.

(b) The effectiveness of management's tactics to sell
     their own ideas while preserving an attempt at
     joint enterprise.

(c) The effects of financial pressures on people,
     built up because of a period of wage restraint,
     that encouraged them to accept even a hard
     bargain.

Secondly, in the face of such considerations, it should be said that Hill's version of the significance of the means by which productivity bargains were struck ('more important than the content of the bargains - significant as that was also') now assumes a rather different connotation than the one he had originally intended. Some genuine attempts at collaboration had been made. Yet despite Hill's faith in the good will of management and the possibility of developing 'a climate of mutual trust and confidence between man and management' it does seem the spirit of trust created by the philosophy and joint working parties was poorly rooted. We do not wish to appear as being unduly critical in saying this. Indeed the factors we have just listed would be considered unexceptional enough in most accounts of wage negotiations. They deserve comment here only to ensure that a balanced view of Shell's productivity bargains may be held. The deal was not an overgenerous one in financial terms. It is a toss up as to whether one chooses to describe the tactics of the management of the day to secure acceptance of the bargains primarily as co-operative and born of a sense of community or as competitive and born of self interest.

THE PRODUCTIVITY DEALS AFTER 1970

Of course it would be unrealistic to expect a large company's management/union relationships fundamentally to change overnight. Subsequent events, however, suggested to many people that the elements of partnership that had characterised preparations for the productivity deals were not to last. Soon after the deals had been introduced levels of earning slipped compared to rival employers and remained behind thereafter. Government policies of pay restraint did not help the company, but neither did the company act noticeably in ways designed to ameliorate the problems. It was widely suggested to us that the company could have done a lot more.

An ex-negotiator for the operators said:

'Up till 1969 there had been wage freezes. So
the pressures were great to sign for money.
But many people believed in the deal then
because it was a change in our position and
status in the company, and because the company
assured us "this was not the end, but the
beginning!"

But look at the value of the productivity
deals then, and now! And look at the erosion
of differentials! The company doing nothing
has left a bitter taste. We (operators at
Shell Haven) have had only one strike in all
this time, but that is not due to the company
being good!'

The abolition of paid overtime had ended any
mechanism by which shop floor level employees could
be paid more money short of increasing their annual
salaries. But successive years of pay policy prevented
this latter course of action. And early reviews of
annual salary levels (conducted in 1971 and 1972
between governmental pay policies) produced settlements
described as 'pennypinching'. While Shell's original
deal had made them leaders, within twelve months or so
other companies caught and passed them without
requiring concessions of workers built into Shell's
deals and, importantly, without abolishing paid overtime. 'In the early days the operators made it work'
said a plant manager. 'Then they looked for the
rewards and did not get them'.

A shift supervisor said:

'It went down hill because of pay restraint.
It was not all Shell's fault. But the company
was not seen as trying to get round pay pauses.
The attitude now is "if you want anything"
you've got to pay for it! The tactic is to
break a bit more of the deal off and sell it
back'.

At the time of our survey very little remained of the productivity deals. Two things impressed us. First, in many ways the 'predeal orthodoxy' has been restored although different words now are used to describe it. Accordingly, payments of salaries, previously made monthly, are now made weekly. The system of 'time-off in lieu' instead of paid overtime has almost completely passed away and nowadays the company pays for almost all overtime worked.

Second, in other areas a vacuum now exists where predeal systems were abolished but where the arrangements which replaced them do not work well. For example, we heard how the 'no clocking' arrangements are now exploited by some workers. We heard too how supervisors faced with such abuses and unable to use authoritarian methods to deal with them are uncertain what else they should do. Neither has the introduction of job flexibility stood the test of the times. While the simpler jobs of minor plant maintenance should have been shared by operators and craftsmen now, we were told, operators tend to 'leave well alone' or at least not undertake such work in daylight. They are not altogether certain what they are allowed to do. Management has now withdrawn the craftsmen previously introduced to teams of operators at Stanlow. And we heard how revised job grading systems that were introduced with the deals have not, as things worked out, given the company sufficient leeway to reward work well done or to pay more for jobs more important or irksome than most, and consequently further attention is being given to this matter.

Aspects of the deal still have their supporters. The scheme of group working which allows men a measure of control in arranging their own cover was praised by some people. But successes now are the exception not the rule.

As we have noted before, government policies did not support ideas built into the deals. The deals have come to look strangely 'out of time and context'. It is a matter of judgement what the company should have done (if anything) about this. But it is undoubtedly true that many people, initially proud to have acquired staff status were very soon to feel disillusioned with the company. 'The company has often promised a lot, then given half and even that was to its benefit' said one person we spoke to. It was commented to us also, and surely correctly, that 'If you think the philosophy was about productivity bargaining, then it failed'.

It is clear that the hopes Hill had entertained that the productivity deal would lend support to any new mood of trust and shared approach started by the philosophy exercise, were to come to nothing. Indeed, the reverse is more true. For many people the productivity bargains are now thought of as an object lesson in how misleading the promises of the philosophy had been.

THE NEW REFINERY

As we have previously observed the final main channel by which the company philosophy should be implemented involved the design of a new refinery at Teesport. Commenting upon this Hill (op.cit.) says:

> 'The fact that the company was planning a new refinery on Teeside at the time the development programme started up was seen as a great opportunity to try out its principles in practice on a green field site. It was possible to design the social system whilst the final design for the highly computerised and automated technical system was still emerging and thus to try out the principle of joint optimisation on a grand scale. It also offered the opportunity to build up from scratch an appropriate set of terms and conditions of employment. It was hoped the new refinery would become an ideal organisation towards which the existing refineries could aim'. (p.109)

Later, Hill feels able to state

> 'Undoubtedly, therefore, Teesport had
> succeeded in setting up a new organisation
> which was a practical demonstration of the
> value of the two lines of action embodied in
> the company development programme: the
> creation of commitment to tasks and
> objectives through appropriate job design;
> and the establishment of appropriate terms
> and conditions of employment'. (p.142)

A rather different picture of the centrality of the philosophy for the new refinery at Teesport is however provided by another member of the E.R.P. team. Writing in his M.Sc. thesis Hibbert says:

> 'As something of an aside it is worth
> mentioning the construction of a new refinery
> and the design of a social system for it. It
> is something of an aside because it is
> questionable whether the philosophy process
> had much influence on it'. (p.30)

In our study we first attempted to discover how much influence the company philosophy had had on events at Teesport. From our discussion with personnel at Teesport itself and from careful study of the Hill and Hibbert accounts it appears that while there was contact between members of the Tavistock Institute and the designers of the refinery and while, similarly, the E.R.P. team did hold discussion with the design group neither of these advisory groups was deliberately retained as specialist advisors. Rather, the main influence of the philosophy came from the extent to which key people in the design team felt receptive to the notion of joint optimisation that was being given such an airing in the company at that time. It should be noted that at least two managers who were closely involved in setting up the Teesport operation were themselves highly conversant with the content of the philosophy statement. Therefore there seemed little real need to involve either E.R.P. or the

Tavistock directly. An interviewee at Teesport said:

> 'At Teesport there was no jockeying, trying to
> do what the boss wanted like at Stanlow.
> Everything was new. The new manager told us
> "its up to you chaps, you've got to operate
> the refinery!" It was a self help programme.
> There was a lot of contact with the Tavistock
> people but they played a <u>very</u> low profile ....
> The design people did give equal weight to the
> social and technical systems. They also
> emphasised job enrichment, delegation and
> flexibility. And there had been real scope
> for choice in the refinery design. A
> hierarchical system had been possible though
> it would have lacked flexibility ....
>
> .... I felt the Tavistock people were just
> articulating what people had been doing for so
> many years. Though I would say that their
> support of the design ideas lent momentum to
> them and some of the doubters were won over'.

In comparison with the other two Shell refineries
that we visited during the course of our study it soon
became evident to us that in certain respects Teesport
is run on rather different lines. We outline these
differences below. The question we particularly sought
to answer, of course, was: to what extent might these
differences sensibly be attributed to the influence
of the philosophy or to what extent do they rather
reflect the influence of purely local factors?

That there are special factors operating here is in
no doubt. The Teesport refinery is smaller, less
complex, more stable and a more highly automated plant
than are either the Stanlow or Shell Haven refineries.
Further it had at its inception all the advantages of
a 'green field' site providing special opportunities
for recruitment and for the arrangement of special
working conditions and terms of employment. In one
crucial respect this was well exploited by the
refinery's architects. All maintenance work in the

refinery was put out to contract, a decision made without reference to the philosophy and which considerably simplified labour/management relations here compared to the older refineries. These contract workers became very well integrated with Shell employees. The high unemployment on Teeside and the availability of labour from the shipbuilding industry gave the company plenty of scope to employ contract labour for maintenance work.

Turning to the areas where the influence of the philosophy on Teesport might be claimed, these can be discussed under three headings. These are: the processes by which the refinery was set up, the design of jobs in the refinery and the arrangement of working conditions and terms of employment.

Regarding the processes by which the refinery was set up it is clear that the enterprise was launched in a spirit of participation and shared involvement. As Hill notes, supervisors were recruited in 1966 some two years before the refinery came on stream and after a period of training were closely involved themselves in the subsequent recruitment selection and training of operators. Hill reports (p.140) one of the supervisors saying of the experience 'Everyone contributed, it was a wonderful experience and I hope that the marvellous spirit of Teesport today lives on'.

Approaches to the Union also resulted in the emergence of the feeling that Teesport was something special. Negotiations between Shell and the operators Union (The Transport and General Workers Union) had been held at national level since 1952. In the mid 1960's there had been a move for more plant and local bargaining; certainly regarding Teesport there seemed the best promise of success for the ideas the company wished to introduce if plans were delegated to the locality itself. As Hill records, the T. & G.W.U. were contacted at head office to clear the way for local negotiations. It seems to have taken just over a year before (in 1966) the Union said Teesport could be separate from the national agreement. While it

112

appears that certain key officials in the Union were keen on grass roots bargaining others were less so. It was suggested to us that the idea was sold to any doubters on the basis that Teesport was a special case. When local negotiations did take place the direct approach to the Unions from the company was a novel experience for local officials who, as Hill records 'proved receptive to Teesport's ideas and contributed in joint discussions to their development'.

Of the design of jobs at Teesport two aspects are notable. The first reflects the sentiment of the philosophy to allow people scope to control their own work endeavours which was welcomed by the operators. It was decided not to appoint charge hands or foremen over operating teams but to require people to report directly to the shift superintendent. By 1970 this system was abandoned as assistant supervisors were appointed. We were told in our study that in fact the originally designed system never had worked in practice and a series of technical problems, the problems of co-ordinating activities across shifts and a major fire necessitated the formal abandonment of the original system. Nevertheless although we were not able to study this point in detail, we were told that some of the original notions to provide enriched jobs for operators still remain.

The second reflects the intention expressed in the philosophy statement to allow people scope to develop in their jobs. At the time of Teesport's start up operators were graded on a seven point training scale. By about 1970 it became clear that the system was not working well and as more operators than were required pressed to achieve a high grading the Company found it was paying for greater flexibility than it required. Subsequent modifications were introduced and today a four point scheme is in operation. It was suggested to us that this reduced the scope for able men to expand their skills (for a period only a proportion were allowed to reach grade four although this restriction was later withdrawn) and that the scale could usefully be expanded.

A number of unusual features for Shell operators was
built into the terms of employment for Teesport
employees. The basic notion was to introduce single
status employment for all of the refineries.
Accordingly, staff were to be paid an annual salary,
there was to be no clocking, no payment for overtime
and so on. In such respects things have not changed
by 1977 although most had, at some stage or other been
considered for change. In other respects the notion
of 'single staff status' for all employees seems to
have been understood to refer simply to the reluctance
of Teesport management 'to introduce differences
between employee groups which in their view are
unjustified'.

Returning therefore to our main task of deciding
to what extent the unusual features of the organisation
of Teesport refinery reflect the influence of the
philosophy our general conclusion is as follows. While
it is impossible precisely to delineate the exact
boundaries of its influence in our view it did not lead
to any spectacular innovations. People may have been
sensitised to the importance of participation in the
introduction of employees to the new plant, yet given
the difficulties and excitements of any new venture
like building a new refinery it hardly seems to us
that this is unusual. Also the efforts to design jobs
on new lines suffered setbacks. And efforts to reduce
unnecessary distinctions between office staff and
operators, while praiseworthy, even ten years ago,
hardly appear revolutionary.

In conclusion, therefore, while the philosophy
probably was of some help to the architects of the
refinery and (at least with respect to terms and
conditions of employment) more of its spirit remains
here than in Shell's older refineries we saw little
evidence to suggest to us that it led to the emergence
of much that was exceptional.

NOTES

(1) Especially, Hill refers to efforts made to ensure the practicability of proposals included in the bargains, and to attempt to secure the support of both supervisors and shop floor people for their implementation.

(2) The exception to this was the JPW involving craft unions at Shell Haven. As we note below the craftsmens' representatives there were suspicious of the JWP idea. This working party was abandoned after a few weeks.

PART III

INTERPRETATION AND SIGNIFICANCE

7　Evaluations

During the conduct of our research we did of course
refer to published accounts of the development of the
philosophy programme (Hill, 1971, Burden, 1975 and
Taylor, 1972). Yet in terms of the evidence we were
collecting, it very soon became clear that these
accounts all offered largely uncritical descriptions of
what took place although they did all differ in their
comprehensiveness and depth of analysis. We became
increasingly concerned at the inconsistency between the
data that we had uncovered in our interviews and these
published accounts. We were curious as to how these
other commentators had come to such different conclusions from those we were beginning to draw, and
furthermore we were worried at the apparent acceptance
within the social science community of the view that
the Shell programme represented a successful social
scientific intervention. This latter impression has
been aided by, for example, Walton (1975) and Trist
(1978) who comment upon the project in favourable
terms. And as we have already noted, Hill, in the
second edition of his book published in 1976, in no
significant way questions his original generally
complimentary conclusions.

   In this chapter therefore we intend to concentrate
upon the ways in which our analysis of the outcome of
the Shell report differs from that of more optimistic
commentators, to justify our analysis in the face of
methodological and other possible objections, and to
juxtapose our own conclusions with those of Paul Hill
and Michael Foster of the Tavistock Institute of
Human Relations who have kindly agreed to include here
commentaries upon our study.

A SUMMARY OF FINDINGS

We have already noted how various other social

scientists have commentated favourably upon the Shell
philosophy programme. In general there is agreement
in such commentaries and evaluations that the project
was innovative and well ahead of its time, that it
represented a successful social scientific intervention, and that the initial main objectives of the
programme, on the available evidence, were broadly
realised. The conclusions we have drawn are somewhat
different and may be summarised as follows:-

(1) Despite the uncritical reports of its
     apparent success, the project never
     really 'took off' and in a number of
     important respects soon faded away.

(2) Top management and their social science
     advisors had somewhat different aims and
     expectations for the exercise.

(3) In terms of the manifest aim of the
     Tavistock workers, to change the philosophy
     of management in Shell UK, the project
     was a failure.

(4) In terms of the implicit aim held by
     Shell's top management, to restore the
     effectiveness of their call to collective
     effort, an evaluation is less straight-
     forward. Despite the broad failure to
     introduce long term change, certain
     benefits did accrue to the company.

(5) The change strategy was ill-conceived
     and also poorly executed. It led to a
     betrayal of peoples expectations.

(6) The developments in this case lead one
     to question the quality of the ideas
     incorporated in the philosophy programme
     and their appropriateness for a company
     like Shell.

We have summarised in Figure 7.1 the data from which we draw these conclusions. It is however important to re-emphasise at this point that whilst these findings and conclusions do suggest that inappropriate change strategies were employed in the project, the real significance of this analysis concerns the reasons why Shell adopted the philosophy programme in the first place and the evolving functions which applied social science came to serve within the company. We return to this issue in the final chapter but before that it is necessary to offer some further justifications for our conclusions to date.

In particular we shall comment upon the claim that the influence of the philosophy is alive today albeit in ways which are difficult to formalise or quantify and that the methodology employed in this study may be insufficiently robust to justify our somewhat sweeping conclusions.

TEN YEARS AFTER

During the course of our research it was pointed out to us by several respondents, and very forcibly by a few, that the whole philosophy programme must have had some effect upon a company which traditionally had been managed in a characteristically paternalistic and authoritarian manner (see chapter three). Some people were impressed by the philosophy and left the early conferences with raised hopes for the future. For some people the project did encourage people to re-evaluate their existing management practices. It is certainly very difficult to evaluate the significance of such events and to balance them against the more pessimistic or negative aspects of this case. Two additional sources of data may help in that judgement. First of all we were able to interview, in 1977, eight people who had joined the company after the philosophy had been launched or had rejoined the company after some years away sometime after 1965. Their observations

Figure 7.1 Summary of findings

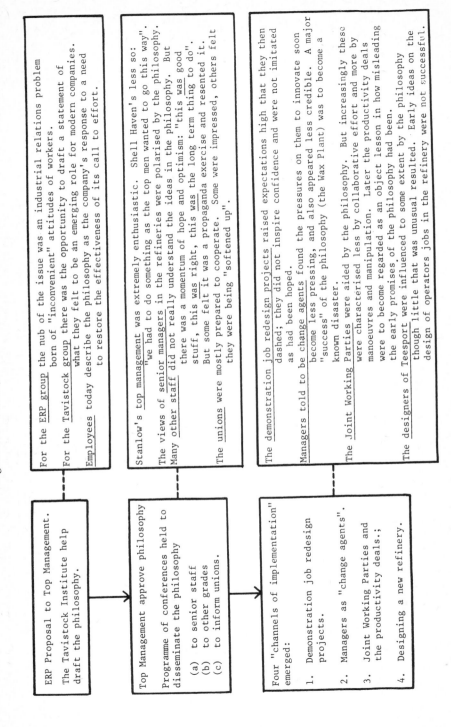

ERP Proposal to Top Management.

The Tavistock Institute help draft the philosophy.

Top Management approve philosophy

Programme of conferences held to disseminate the philosophy

(a) to senior staff
(b) to other grades
(c) to inform unions.

Four "channels of implementation" emerged:

1. Demonstration job redesign projects.

2. Managers as "change agents".

3. Joint Working Parties and the productivity deals.;

4. Designing a new refinery.

For the ERP group the nub of the issue was an industrial relations problem born of "inconvenient" attitudes of workers.

For the Tavistock group there was the opportunity to draft a statement of what they felt to be an emerging role for modern companies.

Employees today describe the philosophy as the company's response to a need to restore the effectiveness of its call to effort.

Stanlow's top management was extremely enthusiastic. Shell Haven's less so: "we had to do something as the top men wanted to go this way".

The views of senior managers in the refineries were polarised by the philosophy. But many other staff did not really understand the ideas in the philosophy: "this was good stuff, this was right, this was the long term thing to do".

There was a momentum of hope and optimism:

But some felt it was a propaganda exercise and resented it. Some were impressed, others felt they were being "softened up".

The unions were mostly prepared to cooperate.

The demonstration job redesign projects raised expectations high that they then dashed; they did not inspire confidence and were not imitated as had been hoped.

Managers told to be change agents found the pressures on them to innovate soon become less pressing, and also appeared less credible. A major "success" of the philosophy (the Wax Plant) was to become a known disaster.

The Joint Working Parties were aided by the philosophy. But increasingly these were characterised less by collaborative effort and more by manoeuvres and manipulation. Later the productivity deals were to become regarded as an object lesson in how misleading the early promises of the philosophy had been.

The designers of Teesport were influenced to some extent by the philosophy though little that was unusual resulted. Early ideas on the design of operators jobs in the refinery were not successful.

give us some idea of the persistence within the company
of the central ideas of the philosophy.

First, some comments from Stanlow:

'Commitment was patchy, ranging from hypnotism
to total scepticism. The majority were in
favour or did not oppose it. Commitment was
highest at the top levels and from those happy
to deal in concepts'. (A senior manager at
Stanlow, who joined in 1969).

'It was talked about cynically. People who
had been initially in favour felt they had
been let down. Few graduates felt it really
existed. Many people who had been to the
original conferences felt conned and doubted
if it had been worth all the effort. The
philosophy was still discussed, but people
felt it was finished'. (A plant manager at
Stanlow, who had joined in 1970).

'I had heard on the grapevine about the
philosophy - that older managers were
suspicious, the younger dubious but prepared
to give it a chance. The climate had been
experimental I'd heard. But I'm not sure
how much was really going on. The biggest
experiment had been in the Wax plant. We'd
had to pick up the pieces there after it had
been exploited for people's own gains.
There's not much of the philosophy left'.
(A senior manager at Stanlow, who had joined
in 1973).

'I was in this job over a year before I first
heard of the philosophy. I've not read it,
there's no pressure to. It's not talked about'.
(A senior manager at Stanlow who had also
joined in 1973).

Comments from Shell Haven:

'When I came back I was very impressed with the changes here. The productivity deal had been a massive step forward .... I was disappointed no-one discussed the philosophy with me and said "that's the way we want to go!"'.
(A middle manager at Shell Haven, who had rejoined the company in 1971 having left at the time of the very bad atmosphere following the 1964 rundown).

'The company philosophy was discussed for a day in a two week induction programme when I joined straight from University. It was just the philosophy they put over, there was no mention of successes or shortfalls with it. Then later I heard that the fundamental concept of enrichment had found few detractors. But there had been a hard sell process at the conferences. It had given a moral uplift to some. But other people had mistrusted "the gleam in people's eye" and anyway, not everyone wants to be a generalist in a team. My own view was that the technical jargon had bemused people'. (Graduate recruit at Shell Haven, who had joined in 1971).

'When I returned in 1972 there was nothing really left of the company philosophy. I couldn't see much. Though I may not have looked too hard. There had been so many changes'. (A senior manager at Shell Haven who had left in 1968).

'My boss gave me a copy of the company philosophy when I joined. I'm not sure why, except they believe in the written word here. He told me not to take it too seriously'.
(A junior manager at Shell Haven who had joined in 1974).

Our second source of evidence on the present day
influence of the philosophy programme comes from our
analysis of the status of social science as an activity
within the two main refineries.

At Stanlow we were repeatedly provided with evidence
of the poor reputation of social science now in the
Refinery. Of all the locations of the philosophy
exercise the project was most visible here.
Undoubtedly, peoples' views were polarised during the
height of the activity here, and later as the project
lost momentum the let-down was marked. 'There must
be a good social scientist somewhere' one manager
remarked. 'I'm fed up with taking part in social
scientific experiments' said another.

At Stanlow also it was clear that while a number of
projects had been undertaken subsequent to the run down
of the exercise no further concerted effort to effect
fundamental change had been made here. What work has
been done at Stanlow was miscellaneous and has been
confined within limited parameters. We present our
report of this work under the headings of job redesign,
the employment of social scientists, management by
objectives and 'other benefits'.

Despite the disappointments associated with the early
work on job redesign at Stanlow that we recorded in
chapter four, some activity in this area continued for
a short while. Following the development of simplified
procedures for undertaking socio-technical analysis a
number of projects were undertaken at Stanlow in 1968
and 1969. The first was unsuccessful and was abandoned
after only a short period. Two others were more
successful, (see Hibbert, op.cit.). In 1969 also,
using Herzberg-type methods, job enrichment was undertaken of supervisors' jobs in a number of departments.
All these projects were considered valuable, though
they did not inspire imitators elsewhere in the
refinery.

At the time of our study no professional social
scientists were employed by the refinery. Prior to

125

this time, however, two social scientists had
successively been employed. It is noticeable that each
of these had been relatively junior level appointments
working on the whole with junior level staff (one
concentrating on work with supervisors, another on
social skills training at junior management level).
The impact of their work was not widely felt and
increasingly it appears top management held them 'at
arms length'. A senior manager told us:

> 'we no longer employ a social scientist here
> - deliberately. We don't know how to use
> them'.

The later Tavistock inspired job redesign work had
emphasised the need for management by objectives in the
refinery. This still continues.

Regarding any 'other benefits' that can be attributed
to the exercise it is correct to record that, much as
the philosophy seems at Stanlow to have polarised
opinion from the start, the presence or absence of
significant long term benefits is a matter of disagreement in the refinery. Yet while many people focussed
only on the disappointments of the exercise some
people certainly did pay tribute to the personal
significance of the philosophy for their own thinking,
pointing out that the programme could be regarded as
a massive management education exercise. Several
people believed the philosophy marked a break with the
company's paternalistic past. The most outspoken
defendant of the exercise at Stanlow said:

> 'it says much for such a programme's durability
> that there is a high level of participatory
> style and awareness of motivating factors such
> that we can ride the storms of Government
> Incomes Policies to the extent that has been
> possible'.

This view, however, was in our experience somewhat
unusual.

At <u>Shell Haven</u>, just as at Stanlow, the comments of many people we spoke to suggested the philosophy exercise for them was something of a 'nine-days wonder'. A middle manager said, for example,

> 'for the first six months everyone said "good morning" to you — trying to meet the objectives of participation. Then it all fizzled out'.

Yet a major difference between Shell Haven and Stanlow was that in the early days of the philosophy not so much had been promised here. At Shell Haven, as we described in chapter 4, top management were more cautious in their approach than had been the case at Stanlow. Consequently opinions had not been polarised to such a degree and while disappointments undoubtedly were felt as the exercise fizzled out the 'let down' was not as severe.

It is interesting to note therefore that at Shell Haven, more than at Stanlow, there is evidence today of some continuity with the philosophy exercise. At this refinery while there was no concerted job redesign programme and while the refinery never drew in professional social scientists from outside onto its staff there is nonetheless reason to believe more lasting benefits may be seen.

The reasons for this do not lie in the institutional-isation of the philosophy's concepts at Shell Haven. Just as at Stanlow, there is very little tangible evidence here of any broad culture change. As one Shell Haven manager put this point:

> 'there have been no general improvements in communication or participation following the philosophy. It all depends on the character of the particular manager or supervisor. <u>Some</u>, a few, managers did become more con-cerned for their staff as a result of the exercise and this remains'.

The main reason why some continuity with the philosophy is today to be seen at Shell Haven is because certain key management positions are presently occupied by individuals whose thinking was deeply influenced by the original philosophy programme.

In the early days of the philosophy launch at Shell Haven a 'Resources Manager' was appointed from within the refinery's staff. The job involved a wide brief, broadly involving a coordination of employee development to planned changes in the technical system of the refinery. Early on this Resources Manager was closely involved in running the philosophy conferences. Later (1969) he helped introduce a management by objectives programme that with fading managerial support had limited success only. In 1972, however, a new refinery manager was appointed who had himself been very influenced by social scientific approaches following his own earlier involvement in the philosophy programme. A working relationship was struck between the two. Some three years later an increasing expectancy that the board of Shell UK would be requiring manpower reductions provided a turning point. Aware that, given the history of Shell Haven, this could not be achieved by conventional methods the Refinery Manager made a positive statement to his top management group that (as we were told) 'the challenges facing Shell Haven should be handled by all the knowledge and resources available, including an understanding and application of "organisational development" concepts'. At the time of our survey a series of over fifty meetings of the top Refinery management team had been held in an effort to do just this.

This development represented the most tangible positive legacy of the original philosophy exercise we encountered. A time consuming team development exercise was in progress that owed something to the original philosophy exercise. Given the coincidence of certain circumstances (the appointment of a Resources Manager, his development and long tenure in the job - the appointment of a Refinery Manager personally affected by the problems) a potentially

significant application of behavioural science ideas
was continuing in at least one of the company's main
refineries. As a footnote, however, it does seem
appropriate to ask whether the same outcome could not
equally have been achieved in some other way, and to
point out that this exercise is to make 'best use of
the company's human resources' and is not directed
towards changing the company's role in society in the
manner of the original philosophy exercise. And whilst
we did find evidence that some individuals had been
personally influenced by the philosophy, we feel sure
that these are a small minority.

A NOTE ON THE METHODOLOGY

It is clear that a retrospective study of the type
reported here does present methodological problems.
In this particular case it seems especially important
to comment on them, as the data are so very damaging
to suggestions that the new philosophy might have come
anywhere near to being adopted in practice in the
company.

   Three possible sources of bias seem particularly
important. The people we spoke to and upon whose
evidence the report substantially depends may have
been unusually anti the philosophy programme.
Additionally, the evidence from interviews concerning
events of some years previously may have been
unreliable and could be misleading. It is also
possible that our report is biased and presented in an
overly critical fashion.

   Regarding the first of these points, in the first
instance, it should be noted that we asked Shell if it
could be arranged for us to speak to people with
knowledge of the philosophy exercise and to have
included in this group some people believed to be
supportive of the philosophy and some thought to be
critical of it. Later, to follow up contentious
issues or ones we felt it necessary to explore further,
we asked for a number of additions to this list, and

we also sought to speak to a few people who had joined
the company after the launching of the philosophy to
build a picture of how perceptions of the programme
had been passed on. In many cases there was little
doubt who it was important to speak to, key actors in
the drama of the philosophy exercise had to constitute
the backbone of our interviewees. But the people who
advised us who to see were themselves still very
interested in the philosophy. They certainly had no
intention themselves to prod us into preparing an
'anti-report' by introducing us predominantly to
critics of it. (Later, their reactions to a draft of
our research report left us, indeed, in no doubt ,at all
on this point).

   On the other hand many of the people who we were
introduced to were pleased to be able to 'let off steam'
to us about the exercise. Many more were keen to put
the record straight, as they saw it. While it was not
our intention to undertake an opinion survey of what
Shell's employees thought of the programme, as our task
was to reconstruct a case study of events associated
with the philosophy, nonetheless this generally
critical mood towards it was unmistakable.

   Noticeable also was the consistency in different
peoples reports of the main themes of the story. Of
course there was room for debate amongst our interviewees of the accuracy of certain details in the
story. For example, different views might be expressed
about precisely when middle managers gave up acting as
agents for change or about what exactly had gone wrong
at the Wax Plant. But around points of more basic
importance to our study there was little or no disagreement at all. To take the same examples, there
was not disagreement about the fact that middle
managers did mostly give up the attempt to introduce
radical changes quite early on. Nor do people doubt
that, rightly or wrongly, the Wax Plant was to become
widely thought of as 'the be-nice philosophy coming
unstuck'. Consistency such as this, taken with the
fact we had no reason to suspect we had been led
towards a grossly biased group of people to talk to,

gives us confidence in the broad accuracy of what we were told.

Regarding our own biases, to the extent that our studies have led us to certain conclusions it would be foolish to say we have a completely open mind now. But to begin with we had no particular axe to grind. Initially in fact we approached Shell for facilities to study only the job redesign work associated with the programme. It was Shell management who impressed upon us the need to look at the broader philosophy exercise if we were to understand any of its particular off-shoots. Indeed it came as a series of surprises to us to learn just what had actually happened in the story of the philosophy programme. In presenting the data we hoped, by using quotations from the interviews, to convey something of the impact on us of what we had heard to the reader of this case report.

Nonetheless, despite care in interviews and in preparation of the research report we did reach conclusions which inevitably must have influenced the reports final presentation. At this point we decided systematically to open these to debate. A draft report was sent to people we expected might disagree with what we said as a preliminary to discussing it with them. In the main this involved people who would have been most distressed by presentation of inaccurate work. This included, amongst others, our contacts in the refineries who had arranged interviews for us, our contacts at Head Office, people at the Tavistock Institute and Paul Hill.

Reactions to the draft report were very varied. Probably everyone was impressed with just how gloomy a picture did emerge when all the different disappointments were discussed in sequence, but some people in the company were angry with us (it was suggested at one point we were anti-Shell) while others felt our perceptions were legitimate enough and should be treated accordingly. In any case, as a result of discussions about the draft report we were able to identify occasional inaccuracies in it and to prepare

what we felt was a more balanced report in consequence.
This is not to say, of course, that the case as now
presented necessarily meets with widespread approval in
the company. Responsibility for the report is ours
alone.

   This being the case and despite (or because of) our
confidence in the accuracy of our report, it seemed
sensible to obtain, if possible, alternative views to
our own to present alongside them. We had no desire to
be open to the criticisms that whereas earlier
published work on Shell's philosophy was generally
positive our retrospective analysis was unwarrantedly
and one-sidedly negative!

   As there is no official 'company view' in Shell on
the philosophy incident it came as a disappointment but
no real surprise that our invitation for a commentary
on our research to be prepared by a company representative was turned down. However, Paul Hill himself
(now no longer with Shell) did agree to comment on our
research, as did Michael Foster of the Tavistock
Institute. Because of work commitments neither was
able to prepare as detailed commentary as he would have
liked but, nonetheless, their comments do highlight
the controversial nature of our research in Shell.
We are very pleased indeed to print here their views.
They will, we are sure, be of assistance to the reader
in making up his or her mind about the significance of
the events we have reported.

COMMENTS BY MICHAEL FOSTER
(Tavistock Institute of Human Relations)

Dear Frank and Colin,

   I have read your paper on Shell's philosophy project
again, and this resulted in my experiencing somewhat
different feelings. It elicited, as before, a certain
amount of nostalgia as well as a similar conviction
that the positive contributions of those most closely
associated with the programme go largely unacknowledged.

(As an aside, organizational change projects present a challenge to the capability and values of those committed. Putting 'the self' at risk offers deep satisfaction as well as anxiety and calls for an element of heroism). What was different about my second reading of your papers was surprise that so much was attempted in the Shell project, and - in its time - how remarkable it was!

Had you for instance chosen to employ a different evaluative stance - even with the same data - I fail to see how it should not have been possible to have arrived at a quite different conclusion. Take point (5) on page 120 for instance, you could have reminded the reader of how little <u>was</u> known and even now <u>is</u> known about change processes in large organisations. But accepting this paucity of knowledge, how the most forward looking aspects of what <u>was</u> known as well as the values associated with organisational survival in the community, were utilised. Certainly a good case can be made out that what was attempted was not 'ill conceived and poorly executed!' In any event, it would have been useful had you spelt out what could be learned from what transpired. What I dislike most of all, perhaps, is your next sentence on the betrayal of people's expectations. That seems to me to be far too sweeping. I suspect that for quite a number of people, the opportunity for considering those fundamental values about the individual, business enterprises and the community, which the conferences provided, was a worthwhile learning experience - and not forgotten.

Another point, so far as I am aware, is that Shell has always been disinclined to employ social scientists qua social scientists. Those who join Personnel Departments almost invariably find themselves fulfilling the usual personnel functions. Again, neither the managers nor that part of the workforce whom I met were ever starry-eyed about social science. The 'exact scientists' - and Shell of course has many - exuded what they called 'a healthy cynicism'. (Which was all very well, but to a partial believer such as myself, somewhat hard to bear). As to the supposition that the

philosophy programme has held up the conversion of
Shell to social science, I consider this problematical.
Personally I doubt it!

In retrospect the dynamics of the Shell project were
extremely complicated. What of the different values
and objectives of the interest groups involved? What
kinds of explanations might be given - in psycho-
analytical terms or others - of the 'negotiations' for
the transfer of power and authority, and the resulting
feelings and effects on the change process? What
impact did the Shell project have on the social science
practitioners' network? Finally, what part has the
programme played in the development of a new paradigm
of work, if one takes a worldwide perspective? (Just
one example, see 'Shell Canada', and their 'Philosophy
Statement'!)

You may have guessed by now this letter represents an
apology for not being able to write a chapter for your
book. Your research paper raises a number of fundamental issues which cannot be dealt with without considerable thought, and unfortunately I am at present
over-burdened with work which is already past its
completion deadline. Ahead there stretches a further
task which must be tackled in the next two to three
months. I am very sorry about this.

Kind regards.

Yours sincerely,

Michael Foster,
28 September 1979.

COMMENTS BY PAUL HILL
(Director, Human Relations Division, MSL Group)

Although not involved in their research in any way, I
was pleased (as one of the originators of the Shell UK

project) to be invited by the two authors to comment on their research paper. I have also accepted their invitation to be frank, although nothing I say should be taken to imply any personal disrespect to Mr. Blackler or Dr. Brown.

Having lived through the Shell UK project, having seen the extensive positive changes which it produced, having experienced - along with many others - the enormous new learning opportunities it provided, I found my overall reaction to the research paper was one of great disappointment.

Whilst the data they have provided from their interviews with existing staff is very interesting and informative, the conclusions they have drawn appear very negatively biased, academic and blinkered.

This impression is created very early in the paper: even their choice of a title (1) is I think, significant: it sets a tone of cynical, rather mocking condescension. Then, in the introductory pages are presented the authors' four main conclusions (2), all negative, which can be summarised as:

(1)   the Shell UK project never really 'took off' and soon faded away

(2)   management and consultants had different aims and expectations

(3)   the change strategy was ill-conceived and poorly executed

(4)   lack of success in the project gave social science a poor reputation in Shell UK.

Time constraints, and pressure of other work, have made it impossible for me to produce the detailed and fundamental critique which I feel these conclusions call for. My comment is accordingly limited. Certainly the first three conclusions do not seem to be supported by the data. Indeed, their interview data

(admittedly from a small selected sample of staff)
seems on the whole to confirm the picture of the project which was already emerging when my book was
written in 1971. There is confirmation of many
(although not all) of the successful achievements (for
example on pages 67, 69, 70, 99, 101, 105, 124, 126,
127, 128). There is also confirmation and elaboration
of the negative aspects which, as pointed out in my
book, were already in 1970/71 threatening the future
of the project.

The research paper makes it clear that the answer to
the question posed in my book in 1971 - whether the
values and concepts of the project were sufficiently
well embodied in the organisation to withstand future
setbacks - must be 'No'. To conclude from this, however, that the whole project was a failure, 'ill-
conceived and poorly executed' is in my view completely
unjustified and unacceptable.

Such a conclusion, I assume, can only stem from the
authors' academic frame of reference, and from their
lack of practical experience in industry, which has
perhaps made it impossible for them to understand the
full significance of the tremendous improvements which
resulted from the project. I will not list these
improvements here, since they are detailed in my book.
One example from the research paper may suffice: the
middle manager's comments quoted on page 124: 'When I
came back (to Shell Haven in 1971) I was very impressed
with the changes here. The productivity deal had been
a massive step forward'.

A more balanced conclusion would be, I suggest, that
the approach adopted in the Shell UK project was
clearly perceived by a minority of people (the
'critical mass' necessary to initiate change) as a
valid and appropriate guide to improving the utilisation and development of human resources in the
organisation, and, as a consequence, to improving its
performance. The majority 'in the middle' were willing
to go along with the change process, whilst a minority
were opposed to it.

So far as the execution of the project was concerned, there were of course mistakes. Perhaps the most obvious were the initial pilot projects, high-lighted in the research paper, but already identified in my book as mistakes. The important thing is that appropriate lessons were learned, other smaller-scale projects were successfully carried out, and a new streamlined form of socio-technical analysis was developed, which was to be widely valued and used in the United States and elsewhere.

For people who, like managers and consultants, are really concerned with winning long-term improvements in industrial or commerical performance, the critical need is surely to build on success, to learn from mistakes, to strive continuously to move forward in spite of inevitable set-backs. In the Introduction to the 1976 reprint of my book, I did, for example, suggest ways in which a 'Shell-type' project could be simplified and improved in order to avoid some of the problems and mistakes of the Shell UK project.

I would like finally to enlarge a little on what I termed the 'blinkered' nature of the research paper. It would seem that whilst the authors are advocating the dustbin for the concepts of the Shell UK project, they are insufficiently aware that .this approach to organisational improvement, based on a philosophy statement, has sparked off great enthusiasm and similar endeavours in many parts of the world, both inside and outside Shell. I will quote only one recent example in Shell Canada.

A new 200 million dollar chemicals plant has been brought on stream in 1978 at Sarnia, Western Ontario. In the design of this plant equal weight was given to the social system and the technical system. A Task force prepared a philosophy statement which, like the Shell UK document, reflects the belief that people will not feel committed to their work unless they are able to meet specific psychological needs through carrying out their jobs.

That the Canadians have built upon the success of the
Shell UK project is obvious. An innovation at Sarnia
of great importance (going significantly beyond what
was achieved at Teesport) was the involvement of the
union right from the start in the planning process.
The result has been a collective contract which
'reflects the intention and objectives of the philosophy statement. Consistent with the assumptions of
trustworthy, responsible employees capable of self-
regulation, the agreement is a very thin document -
only 6 pages versus 45 for its counterpart in the
adjacent refinery with the same union local' ('Shell
World' - October/November 1978).

I hope these brief comments will be sufficient to
convince readers of the research paper that what was
attempted and achieved by the Shell UK project should
not lightly be 'written off'. A far more likely
historical judgement, in my view, will be that it
represents a very significant milestone in the
continuing struggle to create conditions in which
people in organisations will be motivated to work more
effectively and productively.

Paul Hill,
August 1979.

NOTES

(1)   'Whatever Happened to Shell's New Philosophy of
      Management?'

(2)   In the original research paper the conclusions
      were presented in an introduction and not, as
      here, following the case report.

8   Lessons for the 1980s

In this final chapter we set out to draw certain
general conclusions from the Shell story. Rather than
specifically considering the various points of
criticism raised in the final section of the previous
chapter we have chosen to present our review of the
Shell project in a broader perspective. Thus, as a
prelude to discussing its relevance for present day
social science, we consider the ideas that guided the
project in the context of the development of relevant
social scientific notions and in their contemporary
social contexts.

To begin this discussion it is appropriate to note
that ever since Kurt Lewin's achievements demonstrated
to social psychologists in the 1940's that their work
could contribute significantly to practical problems
as well as to theoretical ones (see Marrow, 1969),
good theoretical work of demonstrable practical
significance has been highly prized by such scientists.
Yet Lewin's hopes in the USA (as with those of Myers
in the UK) have not been met in this respect. The
years since the last war have not recorded
psychologists to be assuming an increasing importance
in the formulation of social policies, nor has
academic psychology taken as its main focus the
development of theories relevant to problems of everyday life. Thus, for example, action research, a
technique pioneered by Lewin and his contemporaries to
combine attention to pure and applied scientific
issues, has not been widely adopted. It took indeed
Sanford's 1970 paper 'Whatever happened to action
research?' to prompt Foster (1972) to identify that
despite its low profile certain groups were, still,
using this approach. People working in the field of
'organisation development' (O.D.) have developed
techniques that resemble action research it is true.
But even here, as Kahn (1974) notes, theory development has been slight and Alderfer (1976) in a very

139

optimistic review of the state of O.D. (writing some thirty years after Lewin's death) is only able to say that practical concerns now threaten to influence theory development. This threat has not, certainly, made much impact on undergraduate courses in psychology (see for example comments in Armistead, 1974). Nor, indeed, is it possible to point to many substantial successes even when psychologists have directed their attention to significant social issues (Tizard, 1976).

Against this background of depressed hopes, the Shell project and the tradition of work of which it is a part appear both impressive and attractive. This developing tradition contains, indeed, an unusually long list not only of theoretical achievements but of practical ones also. This, as we saw in chapter 2, includes an articulation of theories through which key social problems may be identified, the development of new practices to cope with such problems, and the formulation of a theory concerning the diffusion of innovations which has been put to use in the promotion of such practices.

Martin Rein's (1976) analysis of ways in which social science might make significant contributions to social policies underlines just how impressive these achievements are. Rein concludes that there are

> 'at least three complementary paths that a social scientist interested in normative questions can pursue. There is first the task of freely speculating and developing imaginative stories with normative implications. The art of story telling and advice giving has only begun to be explored. Secondly, there is the related task which explicitly tries to translate stories into a concrete course of programmatic action .... Design unashamedly postulates values and attempts to develop instruments for their fulfilment; indeed this is the essence of good design. Finally, there is the role of social scientist as critic, with its value-critical, theoretically critical

and empirically critical dimensions'. (Rein, 1976)

Rein is suggesting, therefore, that social scientists may make contributions to the conduct of everyday life by developing reasoned criticisms of social life as presently lived, by developing scenarios of what is both possible and desirable within it, and by inventing programmes of action or specifying options available for realising the possibilities revealed by these other activities.

It is clear therefore that what has been developed by Emery, Trist, Herbst and the many other social scientists working in the tradition they helped pioneer, is a package of ideas, techniques and promises which fills these criteria exactly. The idea of the changing nature of organisational environments increasingly characterised by 'turbulence' can be used to interpret many problems of modern society. The notion of 'socio-technical system' helps point out how traditional concentration on technical demands in job and organisational design has led to an underestimation of the importance of social ones. Again, suggestions about the importance of new sets of values to be accepted in society, that companies should adopt roles more adaptive to their environments (i.e. should be more collaborative and less competitive) and that social and technical considerations should be jointly optimised in job design efforts provide a scenario of possibilities to be aimed for. Finally, experience in the problems of persuading others to act on such notions and the development of a theory of diffusion has led to a near political programme of actions (undertaken by the International Institute for the Quality of Working Life, see Blackler and Brown, 1978) designed actively to promote these ideas. Here are all the appearances, of a social movement. Emerging at a time of considerable social changes it combines the authority of a science, with both the ideals of a humanism and the assurances of a technology; moreover it presents also a track record of not inconsiderable practical achievements to back its claims for consideration.

At its best, therefore, the tradition of work of
which the Shell project is a part can appear to be not
only a vindication of the past hopes of applied social
psychologists but, perhaps more importantly, also as a
model of their hopes for the future. Nonetheless, this
very promise does, on closer examination, seem to
contain within it certain dangers. The excitement
associated with such an apparent 'coming of age' of a
branch of applied social science could very easily
lead to a general relaxation in the standards of
criticism and analysis that would normally be
associated with scientific endeavour. Criticisms of
relevant theory may be construed as wilful or as
destructive. For who wants to be told, just as things
appear to be going well, that all is not what it seems
to be and that a scholarly re-analysis may be required
of just those very ideas which are proving so
inspiring in practice? It is far more tempting to
regard failures in particular applications of these
key ideas, not as indicative of shortcomings within the
ideas themselves, but as indicative of clumsy attempts
to apply them. We return to this theme in the
concluding paragraphs of this chapter, turning not to
comment more directly on the ideas themselves which
guided the Shell project.

THE PHILOSOPHY AND FLOWER POWER

At the time when the new philosophy was being introduced to Shell, as we discussed in chapter 2, a very
different movement to change the world was developing
outside. This was the decade of flower power and of
exhortations to make love not war, of psychedelic
drugs and their promises for new ways of seeing, and
of prophets like R.D. Laing with his message the world
was mad and Charles Reich with his prescription that
all that was needed to deal with a crazy world was the
acquisition of 'consciousness III'. Such developments
reached their peak at the end of this decade and marked
a brief period of widespread and heroic optimism in
our society that fundamental changes could be made
immediately if only people would find the courage to

embrace new life styles.

The distinguishing feature of the various cult ideas
of this period was not that their proponents claimed
any special knowledge or expertise. Theirs was simply
a claim that they had achieved a form of wisdom, indeed
the very special and fragile form possessed only by
innocent people. 'Innocence' is, perhaps an easily
misunderstood term for like the term 'ignorance' it
implies certain things are unknown; it should not,
however, be confused with ignorance because, unlike it,
innocence implies less an unfamiliarity with certain
facts and more an unfamiliarity with certain motives.
Innocent people are distinguished by their purity of
purposes, their simplicity, and by the directness of
understanding that they possess as a result.

People involved in the youth movement of the 1960's
self consciously strove to attain such a state. In his
1968 book 'The Making of a Counter Culture' Theodore
Roszak championed this effort:

'However lacking older radicals may find the
hippies in authenticity or revolutionary
potential, they have clearly succeeded in
employing radical disaffiliation - what
Herbert Marcuse has called the Great Refusal -
in a form that captures the need of the young
for unrestricted joy. The hippy, real or
imagined, now seems to stand as one of the
few images toward which the very young can
grow without having to give up the childish
sense of enchantment and playfulness, perhaps
because the hippy keeps one foot in his
childhood .... Is it any wonder that the best
and brightest youngsters at Berkeley High
School .... are already coming to class
barefoot, with flowers in their hair, and
ringing with cowbells?' (Roszak, 1968,
pp.39-40)

Not everyone, however, can share Roszak's evaluation
of flower power. Rollo May, for example, has developed

143

a highly critical analysis of the movement. He does, of course, recognise the power that springs from an approach to life free of guilt and evil intention. Yet he has no time for the self righteous claims of the flower power era. Their form of innocence he does not regard as genuine but as a phenomenon to be dubbed with the term 'pseudo-innocence':

'Capitalizing on naivety, it consists of a childhood that is never outgrown a kind of fixation on the past. It is childishness rather than childlikeness. When we face questions too big and too horrendous to contemplate, such as the dropping of the atomic bomb, we tend to shrink into this kind of innocence and make a virtue of powerlessness, weakness and helplessness. This pseudo-innocence leads to utopianism, we do not then need to see the real dangers. With unconscious purpose we close our eyes to reality and persuade ourselves that we have escaped it. This kind of innocence does not make things bright and clear, as does the first kind; it only makes them seem simple and easy'. (May, 1972, p.49)

Attractive though the intentions of the pseudo-innocent may be theirs is, May points out, a state of mind dangerously non-adaptive to the modern world. Pseudo-innocence is an innocence without responsibility, a defence from facing the realities of power and prestige, for it is composed of the fantasy that just a general love and goodwill will enable everything to be O.K. after all. Pseudo-innocent people are simplistic rather than simple. Their state of mind at best involves a lack of curiousity and at worst a dogmatic assertion that all basic problems are solved by their views.

While the managers of Shell never did turn up for work 'barefoot, with flowers in their hair and ringing with cowbells' (nor, we hasten to add, were they ever asked to!) there are a number of intriguing similarities between flower power and Shell's new philosophy. On the positive side, just as flower power seemed to challenge established authorities, so did Shell's philosophy. Both were naively confident about their self evident validity. Just as flower power undoubtedly did leave a legacy (in attitudes towards women, the environment, and mysticism, for example) so did Shell's philosophy, difficult though it would be to assess either one precisely. Yet more than all those there is, on the negative side, the point that like the flower children Shell's story shows unmistakable signs of 'pseudo-innocence'. For Shell's attempt to introduce the new philosophy implied that simple and easy solutions for some of the most profound organisational and social problems were possible, available indeed just for the taking.

The pseudo-innocence of the philosophy stems from the two core ideas within it. The notions of 'stewardship' on the one hand (through which the organisation was intended to fit better into its environment) and 'joint optimisation' on the other (through which technical and social needs were to be matched) seem to have been formulated with no real appreciation of either the cut and thrust of the oil business or the 'political' (as against social and technical) dimension of organisational management.

Regarding the first of these, the notion of steward-ship, it will be recalled that as one of our inter-viewees explained to us (see p.49) this idea was the foundation of the philosophy statement. Yet, as he continued to explain, it is now apparent that far less people than it first seemed really supported this idea or thought it workable in Shell Refining. His assess-ment on this point was validated to some extent by the somewhat incredulous comment we later received from a senior manager in the company after he had read our draft research report. Commenting on our quotation from this interviewee (this is reproduced in this book on p.49 line 28 to 40) he wrote by way of comment that it:

'seems to indicate by the quote the company
"is the custodian of the assets of society
and should not even make a profit at its
expense" that the management had decided to
give up their managerial role. I find it
hard to believe that this was a stated
attitude of management'.

Whether one thinks this aim for managers to aspire to
involves an abdication of management responsibilities
or not depends, presumably, on how one defines them.
Yet it is certain that the company's new philosophy
purported to be introducing new and significant ideas
in this respect. Indeed, however unlikely it may seem
at first sight that top management in Shell UK Refining
agreed to these new ideas it is a matter of history
that they did. The opening two paragraphs of the
philosophy, in describing the company's 'primary
objective' state:

'Shell Refining Company is primarily concerned
to maximise the contribution to the long term
profitability of the Shell Group insofar as this
arises from the efficiency with which it uses
the Group's resources of men, money and material.

The resource to which it has legal rights of
privileged access are nonetheless part of the
total resources of society as a whole and are,
in this sense, social resources; the Company
believes they must be presented, developed and
managed as such. It furthermore believes that
its use of these resources must be such as to
contribute to meeting society's requirements
for products and services'.

As we have seen before Emery and Trist's analysis of
turbulent environments and the problems associated with
them had led them to postulate a need for large
companies to adopt new roles in society. In their
'Toward a Social Ecology' the case for this was spelt
out with (see p.185 of the book) the Shell story
presented as an example of what could be done.

146

Important among their themes here was a discussion of the need for companies to adopt new attitudes towards the ownership of resources; more specifically of them asking themselves under what conditions they have access to the resources they handle, who else may have legitimate claims to them, and how these various rights might be reconcilable. Consideration of such questions, they argued, would promote a 'new negotiated order' where a mutual accommodation of differing, though legitimate, interests could be talked through.

What seems to be exciting from this account is the suggestion that a company based in one of the world's most important businesses was seriously re-considering its role in such a way. Yet an actual reading of Shell's philosophy suggests this reflection was, in practice, to be contained within certain definite boundaries. The statement we quoted above goes on to recognise, indeed emphasise, the limited freedom of action available to a company locked into a much larger group of companies concerned with the various activities undertaken in the oil business, such as oil exploration, production, transportation, manufacturing and research. Within the philosophy statement certain particular objectives, understood to follow from the company's 'primary position', were then listed. These amount to the surprisingly uncontroversial objectives of low cost refining under conditions where people can exercise their potentials and contribute to the company effort, which are safe, and which do not inter- fere with community amenities. One further operational objective was specified, that the company was committed to:

'seeking continually from the Group the power and the information necessary to enable it to meet its responsibilities .... In certain circumstances it may be necessary to seek a re-definition of its responsibilities in order that the Company's capabilities may be best used on behalf of the Group'. (Please consult Appendix for the full version of the philosophy statement)

Yet excepting whatever scope for a re-definition of company strategy this particular objective allowed, the role prescribed looks singularily unremarkable. Rather than it comprising an experimental blueprint for new roles companies may develop in turbulent environments the philosophy's statement of goals resembles the conventional enough outcomes that might follow, for example, from a management by objectives programme.

Thus the promise of basic developments in the company's social role appears largely to evaporate on close reading of the philosophy itself. Now, a decade and a half after it was written, the implication of what 'stewardship' might imply for an oil company are, perhaps, more clear than they were in 1965. It is evident today, for example, that the overwhelmingly important resource to which any oil company has 'privileged access' is oil itself. It is evident now too that any oil company which was seriously to consider respecting the claims of others to this finite resource would seek to ensure the exploitation of oil in a more or less rational and planned way. Thus, through action regarding prices, availability and distribution, as well as by advising and negotiating with governments and other interest groups it would attempt to balance various social considerations. The issues would by no means be uncontroversial for, arguably, such considerations would include debating the needs of oil producing as well as of oil using states, of the needs of underdeveloped countries, as well as of developed ones, and of the needs of future as well as of present generations for this vital, scarce, and non-renewable resource.

While all this may be clearer now than it was in the mid 1960's it remains true that the new role Emery and Trist had in mind for Shell in particular, or other companies in general, was intended to be something more than a mere call for efficient and careful business activity under acceptable working conditions. Given the recognised limits of what might be possible, with regard to developing new attitudes towards resources in a company like Shell Refining that was

148

locked into a much broader group of oil companies, extra vigilance in pursuit of such a goal might have been thought necessary. Yet, surprisingly perhaps, there is no evidence to suggest this was fully understood. Challenging debating points were undoubtedly posed at the philosophy conferences. Yet no project groups were formed as a result of them to review Shell Refining's broad social role. No special study groups were formed with other companies in the Royal Dutch Shell Group to work through its implications. No special negotiations were opened with interest groups outside. Whereas more than a simple legitimation of the company's existing activities was presumably sought for, quite what it was intended to be is not very clear.

It is our suggestion therefore that while it must have been a heady enough experience to stage manage a series of conferences throughout a company with employees of many levels joined in debate about the contribution of their work to society, the effectiveness of this as a change strategy was limited. As a vehicle for redirecting the company's purposes and relations to external groups and institutions, the programme of conferences was a non-event. The implications of the statement that the company needed to treat the resources it handled with the care and respect due to communably 'owned' resources were not well thought out. The conferences were, indeed, safely insulated from the forces, issues and decision making frameworks which, in practice, determined company actions and strategic policies. From today's vantage point what appears surprising in the philosophy statement is not that it anticipated a radical new role for companies in the modern world but that anyone could have seriously thought that it might have done.

While therefore the idea of 'stewardship' as presented in the philosophy suggests the presence of pseudo-innocence, so also does the philosophy's second key concept. The idea of 'joint optimisation' was, as we have seen, the inspiration of each of the four 'main channels' that emerged to implement the philosophy. Yet here too several points suggest the conclusion that

the philosophy encouraged far too an optimistic view of
what could be hoped for.

   In developing criticisms of the idea of 'joint
optimisation' we do not wish to be understood as dis-
missing out of hand either socio-technical theory in
general or its particular incorporation in Shell's new
philosophy. The reasons for this are that the
philosophy statement (like socio-technical theory) was
unusual in that it strongly emphasised the point that
human needs should receive serious attention in the
theory and practice of organisation, just as
traditionally technological requirements so obviously
have. For technical people, trained exclusively in
engineering perhaps, and for whom the human element in
organisation may appear an unpredictable and untrust-
worthy element, the implications of this insight may,
of course, have been revealing. In addition, the
emphasis in the philosophy on the need to explore new
options in organisation design that might be available
develops the point further. The philosophy itself and
the conferences at which it was discussed despite all
the short comings that our research report has pointed
towards undoubtedly provided an opportunity, previously
unavailable, for people to reflect on assumptions that
they had held about management and to reflect also
about the inevitability of these ideas.

   Yet having made these points it would be denying the
main thrust of our research data to present them too
forcibly. The case study we have reported here
illustrates above all how the expectations generated by
the philosophy programme were to be let down. The
legacy left by the programme is not primarily one of
gratitude that new horizons were opened for people.
Primarily, the philosophy is remembered by the extent
to which its promises of joint optimisation and of a
new deal in man-management approaches proved to be
misleading.

   It will be evident that, in part, this state of
affairs developed because the exercise was, it can now
be seen, badly managed with inadequate resources being

used to back up the efforts that were made or that were encouraged. In the next section we discuss further certain aspects of the change strategy used and its short comings. However regarding our present concern, the nature of the ideas that were the concern of this strategy, it can with the benefits of hindsight be seen also that the strong points of the ideas in the philosophy were, at the same time, its failings. To the extent to which it emphasised the significance of human needs, their relevance for job designs and for management styles, and to the extent it drew attention to opportunities for shared values and benefits, the philosophy was useful and instructive. But in its very success in focussing on these issues it simultaneously failed to illuminate other, and as it turned out, equally important facets of organisational life. The philosophy failed satisfactorily to draw attention to areas of potential conflict between organisational imperatives and personal ones. Emphasising (probably correctly) that much more scope for accommodating both Shell's and its employees needs existed than previously had been recognised the philosophy nonetheless failed to note that other factors than technology mitigated against a wholehearted 'joint optimisation' of them. While Emery and Trist could write of the need for differing interest groups between organisations to negotiate over their various, though legitimate, interests they did not in the philosophy they wrote for Shell recognise the implications of such an analysis for affairs within the company itself.

Thus it was by no chance that the philosophy was entitled a 'management philosophy' and not an 'organisational' one. As such its message was that, using the insights of modern behavioural science, management and employee harmony could be achieved. The safety and security needs of employees were recognised in the philosophy, but the psychology from which all significant action followed emphasised values of achievement, responsibility, and personal growth through work. The doctrine of joint optimisation was, as we have seen, built on this foundation. Yet the employees of Shell, en masse, did not demand redesigned jobs. Managers who tried to adopt more participative styles were not always rewarded by more co-operative staff. The productivity bargains began to look less and less like bargains to those whose salaries were determined by them. These facts, and the highly derogatory views on the philosophy we so often encountered in our research programme suggest that the term 'joint optimisation' in Shell's philosophy could be a candidate for George Orwell's vocabulary of 'Newspeak'. Indeed, we did hear of how one manager said at the end of his philosophy conference that he was going back to his work group 'to optimise the bastards!'

Yet there is, of course, a crucial difference between the outpourings of the Ministry of Truth in '1984' and the intention of the architects of the new philosophy of 1965. The fictional characters in the former were ruthlessly manipulativein their debasement of language; the real characters associated with Shell's philosophy intended no harm in what they were doing, quite the reverse in fact. Like many before them they had assumed that profound organisational and social problems could be solved by better human relations management. In the 1960's they were not alone in their approaches either. Other social scientists were working along lines similar to aspects of socio-technical theory. Thus, organisational theory, influenced by Woodward's research and also by the social upheaval generated by the 'white heat of the technological revolution', was at this time preoccupied with the effects of technology in organisations. Similarily at this time organisational psychology, spurred by the promise of Herzberg's work on the one hand and problems of high absenteeism and turnover on the other, was becoming more and more concerned with job design.

Yet the fact that errors of judgement and emphasis were easily and understandably embodied within the philosophy is no real excuse for the fact they were to be so embodied. Not all social scientists working in

152

organisations at this time – even those sympathetic to socio-technical systems theory – were impressed by the idea of writing a company philosophy like Shell's. One such individual for example, working in Shells' rival Esso, describes how at the time of the philosophy exercise in Shell to their apparent relief she advised Esso managers against such a programme (Klein, 1976, p.47). As we have previously indicated, while purporting to be a more comprehensive affair the philosophy was misleading in that it drew attention only to certain selective and partial aspects of organisational life. Opportunities for co-operation through changes values and more creative job design were emphasised. But not mentioned were the limitations to shared objectives suggested by factors, for example, like the pressure of outside interest groups (e.g. Government inspired pay pauses), the size of the company, its ownership and governance and the differential power bases available to interest groups within it.

It was no accident or mere failure of administration that led to the widespread disappointments associated with the philosophy programme therefore. The organisation theory implicit within it was inadequate, failing as it did to recognise the reality of competitive motivation and unequal opportunities. Employees affected by the philosophy were right enough when they said the philosophy amounted to little more than an exhortation on them to 'be nice' to their staff. With regard to 'joint optimisation', as with other aspects of the philosophy, Shell's programme confirmed the lessons the flower children learned: good intentions are just not enough.

NOTES ON THE CHANGE STRATEGY OF THE PHILOSOPHY PROGRAMME: SOCIAL SCIENCE AS FLUORIDATION

While it may be apparent now that Shell's new philosophy was incomplete, its original proponents in the mid 1960's had no such doubts about it. The very certainty with which they presented their views

153

constituted an important characteristic of the Shell
story. In this section we illustrate how this
certainty led to the particular change strategy
employed in Shell and how this strategy, in conjunction
with the incompleteness of the philosophy just
discussed, led to so many disappointments.

That the Tavistock theorists were sure of their
position is of no surprise. We have already discussed
how their scholarly analysis of social trends, which
pointed to certain alarming difficulties in
organisational management and institutional stability,
and their implicit theory of human nature, which
emphasised peoples needs for opportunity and development, had provided the bases of authority for their
prescriptions. It is easy to see how the central
points of concern for the Tavistock people in the mid
1960's could become less a search for further
theoretical developments and more a search for
efficient ways of disseminating the ideas they had
already formulated. How quickly and successfully
society could begin to adopt the new outlooks and
practices Emery and Trist's analysis suggested were
necessary, as we previously argued, were the problems
concerning them in the Shell project.

In a similar way the ERP unit in Shell saw themselves
as pioneers. Given their challenging task of long term
planning for the industrial relations function of the
company, their studies had led them to modern management theory. Here they found the suggestion that
managerial actions are guided by implicit, though
perhaps only half recognised, assumptions about human
behaviour. Should these be erroneous, e.g. that people
need to be closely controlled or coerced in their jobs,
the implication was that the resulting actions could be
damaging for good industrial relations. Applied to
Shell, this argument suggested that less than ideal
industrial relations in the company were a predictable
consequence of poor management practices. The
priority, therefore, that the ERP unit was concerned
with was how managers in Shell could be educated into
adopting a new philosophy of management that would

guide them quickly towards more appropriate behaviours.

Thus both the Tavistock social scientists and the ERP team in Shell shared a sense of urgency in their work, as for both these groups, albeit for different reasons the philosophy amounted to nothing less than a blueprint for a new order of things. While neither was quite sure how quickly others would be persuaded of the correctness of this nonetheless it seemed that the powers of reason and of the philosophy stood good chances of success and, as it seemed from early indications, were actually winning the day.

The model for social change adopted within Shell was, therefore, analogous to the process of fluoridation. Fluoride added in minute amounts to supplies of drinking water does, it would seem, help to prevent tooth decay. Similarly the new philosophy would, it was hoped, work through the system to nourish parts other medicines could not reach, and would stimulate changes other techniques could not manage!

It was no mere administrative misjudgement then that so little regard was shown for the need for back-up resources to support the job redesign experiments or the exhortation that new management styles should be adopted. It was just not appreciated how necessary they would be. The model for change in the minds of the architects of the philosophy programme led its organisers to expect that the principles they gave to others would permeate the system and lead to their own consequences. Certainly Shell's top management had decided prior to the philosophy that productivity deals should be sought in the company and the Tavistock people also expected that certain job design changes would follow from the philosophy programme. Yet more than these alone were hoped for, for the philosophy was intended to be but the starting point for widespread and developing changes.

Undoubtedly, of course, these expectations were not altogether thwarted. Some individuals were impressed by the philosophy and changed their ways. Others, at

155

Teesport for example, were at the very least reinforced in their plans by the philosophy. But the pseudo-innocence of the philosophy that we discussed in the last section, coupled with the basic naivete that we have just outlined was destined to lead to disappointments. Thus each of the main channels which 'emerged' through which the philosophy was to be implemented led to disappointments. Too much was promised from job redesign, inadequate organisation theory led to unrealistic expectation for managers to be change agents, the experience with the productivity deals contradicted the spirit of the philosophy they allegedly demonstrated, and what developments at Teesport really owed to the philosophy remains uncertain. In terms of effectively lasting changes the philosophy did, indeed, amount to little more than a drop in the ocean.

While the change model of 'fluoridation' in conjunction with the pseudo-innocence of the philosophy led to the failures just listed they also gave rise to a more basic flaw in the philosophy programme. The philosophy was not intended to be used manipulatively by one interest group at the expense of another. It was not the intention of the Tavistock people unfairly or insidiously to manoeuvre people through the philosophy. Yet, in various ways it is clear that manipulation did become an important feature of the Shell programme.

Shell's new philosophy did not, of course, begin with scheming although it can be said to have ended that way. It will be recalled that, in the latter stages of preparing for the productivity deals, finding progress through consultations tediously slow, Shell's industrial relations staff fed ideas into the different working parties with the unions as if they were spontaneously occuring to them. It was as if these apparently new ideas were inspired by 'the spirit of the philosophy'. In truth, however, management had already decided what it wanted and was using the philosophy argument as something of a ploy in order to present its plans acceptably. In our more detailed description of this manoeuvering presented earlier we commented on how contrary this action was to the ideals of respect and participation championed in the philosophy, no matter how successful it may have been in speeding the productivity deals along. But while this episode serves as a reminder of the reality of the industrial relations situation in the company and the problems for genuine participation within it other, more subtle, opportunities for the philosophy exercise to be used manipulatively had been present within it from the start.

A quotation from one of our interviewees will introduce this very important point. This interviewee had been present at the very first discussion of the philosophy with the company's top managers, and he described to us the doubts about the proposed programme he had felt both then and later. He and his refinery manager from Shell Haven found they were much less keen on the philosophy than people from Stanlow had seemed to be:

> 'We were more sluggish getting off the mark than Stanlow was. We weren't sure how to handle it. We had the Tavistock people over for a few days but I blew my top at them! They wouldn't give us an opinion as to what we ought to do. "What are we paying you for?" I exploded! They explained they were working only as catalysts and we had to take responsibilities for any programme'.

While this interviewee went on to say he learned a lot from this episode, his story of it is a revealing one. Non-directive consulting in organisational change programmes has, especially since Argyris's 1970 book, been well known and practised by change agents. Argyris describes the process as the consultant helping people make free and informal choices to which they can feel committed, while at the same time the consultant self consciously avoids the temptation to impose his own analysis and solutions on the people he is serving. While the incident described above (as the Tavistock

people refused to translate their general philosophy
into specific policies) may appear to be an example of
consulting in such a style it is evidently not. All
strategic choices had already been taken by the consultants. The most choice the refinery managers really
had in this case was either to take or to leave this
particular package then on offer; it was not theirs to
fashion in the first place. As the interviewee we
quoted indicated, however, the extent to which the
choice had actually been left to them was equivocal:

> 'We felt we had to do something. The ideas
> had been sold well to the boss of manufacturing.
> We had to do something as the top man wanted
> to go this way. Given free choice I'm not sure
> what we would have done'. (see p.43 of this
> book)

With this background the reality of the situation
appears to have been that this particular individual
found himself presented with a puzzle he had not
devised of which, he was told, it was his choice to
take or leave but which, it was clearly apparent, he
had better solve in the accepted manner anyway. In the
circumstances the fact that he 'blew his top' was quite
understandable!

A similar dilemma to this was also created in the
philosophy conferences themselves. Their ostensive
purpose was to enable people to discuss and freely to
accept or reject the philosophy. Yet, evidence
descriptions nowadays about the 'brainwashing'
allegedly associated with them, some people had doubts
about this! Certain indications, no doubt, suggested
to them that at a fundamental level it was not really
up to the conference participants at all to decide on
the issues. Time provided off work, generous hotel
accommodation, expenses paid, backing for the
philosophy from top management, authority for it from
eminent social scientists, the confidence of the
company officials who ran the discussions, these and
other features were very much in evidence. They would
have suggested to the conference participants that

acceptance of the philosophy if not actually to be
expected, was certainly much to be encouraged.

An additional point concerning pressures on people to
comply concerns the attractiveness of the philosophy
anyway. Within the statement a reconciliation of
potentially troubling problems was apparently achieved.
Thus, profit motive and social service were both used
to justify company activities. Efficient business
management and humanitarian social ideals were made to
appear both compatible and even complimentary. A
potential dissenter to the philosophy therefore would
not only have found the very forum of the conferences
somewhat anti-thetical to the expression of his doubts
but may have found his doubts themselves rather dis-
turbing. Pushed too far they might appear to imply
that Shell's role in society was not without its
problems. Unless an alternative position to the
philosophy's had previously been well thought out, and
could clearly have been presented at the philosophy
conferences, it is clear therefore that criticism of
the philosophy would have been difficult to maintain in
the company of well meaning and company oriented men.
In such circumstances it can hardly be deemed surprising that many who had doubts about the philosophy
appear to have acquiesced in the conference discussions.
Nor is it altogether surprising that some of the people
we spoke to about the conferences in our review of the
programme chose rather bitterly to describe them
several years after the event as 'brainwashing'.

It is our assessment therefore that the opportunity
for misuse of the philosophy was present in the exercise from the start. Despite the good intentions of
the designers the philosophy they promoted was naive
in its promises of social and organisational harmony.
This situation was further confounded by the confidence
and singlemindedness with which they presented it,
convinced as they were of the good they were doing. In
the industrial relations context of Shell in the mid
1960's the outcome of this process was a philosophy
that, rather than heralding a new social order, was of
mere passing utility in helping to re-establish the

legitimacy and effectiveness of management's call to collective endeavour.

FAREWELL TO INNOCENCE

The points we have made in this chapter about the Shell episode may be summarised as follows. The project falls within a tradition in applied social science that is both impressive and appealing. Yet the outcomes of the project suggest that certain rather basic difficulties are associated with the ideas that fashioned its development. The first of these difficulties we have described as the pseudo-innocence of the philosophy programme. Especially, it involved an underestimation of the realities of power structures in the oil industry generally and in Shell UK in particular. The second and related difficulty that we have discussed was the change strategy adopted in the project, analogous as it happened to be to the process of fluoridation. On this point we have shown how the optimism and confidence of the philosophy's supporters led to a let down of their, and others, expectations. Also our analysis showed how this overconfidence combined with the pseudo-innocence of the ideas inspiring the project to lead to certain manipulative elements developing within it.

Since the time of the Shell project there has been a great deal written and spoken about applied social science and undoubtedly now the project looks somewhat dated. Yet in our view the main flaws of the Shell project can be seen today in certain areas of applied social science. To the extent that the ideas which guided the Shell project have also influenced more recent developments this conclusion is unremarkable enough. To the extent also that the mistakes of the Shell project were easily made, this conclusion is likely to have a recurring validity!

Regarding the extent to which the ideas which guided the Shell project have also influenced more recent developments, as our analysis of the social context of

of the ideas built into the Shell project indicated,
many influential and well known notions in the applied
social sciences may be traced to this period. Apart
from the package of ideas associated with the analysis
of turbulent environments and socio-technical systems
that continues to be presented as guidelines for action
there is, of course, the variety of activities which
may be listed under the heading 'organisational
development' (O.D.) whose genesis (see French and Bell,
1973) can also be traced to the 1960's. Much as, in
accord with the mood of the 1960's, the Shell project
was based on a particularly optimistic model of man,
O.D. too (as Tannenbaum and Davis stated in 1969)
assumes people are basically good, trustworthy and
collaborative. Accordingly, as French and Bell's
review makes clear, O.D. is largely concerned with the
creation of conditions to help people communicate more
openly together in a spirit of trust and collaboration.
Such is evidently a commendable thing to do, but (as
the Shell project so vividly illustrated) is also open
to abuse if conducted in disregard of the reality of
competing interests and differential power bases in
business organisations.

Just as we have accused the Shell project of pseudo-
innocence so have others developed criticisms of O.D.'s
naivety. Thus for example Nord (1974) and Stevenson
(1975) have both observed that O.D. approaches do not
acknowledge political and power factors in
organisations, and Alderfer, having recorded how value
dilemmas have increasingly come to worry O.D.
practitioners, went on to say:

> 'At the crux of the value disputes within O.D.
> is the problem of power. O.D. professionals
> must struggle with whether their professional
> competence (power) is being used to advance
> humane values and with whether they can harness
> enough power to bring about desirable change in
> human organisations'. (Alderfer, 1977, p.199)

The problems of pseudo-innocence associated with some
modern presentations of socio-technical theory have

161

perhaps been less well recognised. As we have pointed out elsewhere (Blackler and Brown, 1978) important criticisms of job redesign theory have been developed by social scientists not themselves involved in job redesign practice. These criticisms have, however, passed largely unrecognised by job redesign theorists themselves. Comments by Braverman (1974), Fox (1976) and Nichols (1976) to the effect that job redesign on its own is unlikely to make much significant difference to the quality of workers lives have not prompted much response from socio-technical theorists, a position reminiscent of the situation in the 1960's when Baritz's book 'The Servants of Power' criticising the activities of industrial psychologists was almost totally ignored by them.

Yet some criticism of socio-technical approaches have been recognised by certain people active in developing the approaches further. Two case reports are notable here, both of which confirm the limitations of socio-technical approaches illustrated in our Shell report. Bolweg (1976) reported on a decade of experimentation with socio-technical approaches in Norway, where the creation of semi-autonomous groups of workers was presented as an approach to industrial democratisation. Among his conclusions is the finding that this approach to industrial democracy was severely limited unless used in conjunction with other, broader, approaches and that socio-technical theory itself fails to accommodate the political implications of industrial democracy. A further significant study is Anderson's (1976) review of the problems associated with the introduction of job redesign as part of a programme for industrial democracy in South Australia. In this case too it became clear that more needed to be done than simply relieving monotony at work by job redesign, and the political aspects of industrial democracy quite clearly emerged in this case with the unions first objecting to job redesign being used in isolation from other approaches and the employees later objecting to plans to extent participation to include representation at Board level!

A recognition of the potential for pseudo-innocence of social scientific ideas of the type we have been discussing draws ones attention to a simple, but none-theless significant, truth. The conditions associated with feelings of fulfilment through work may have little to do with the conditions associated with the optimum performance of industrial organisations as conventionally arranged. It is, of course, tempting to believe that the conditions of optimum worker productivity are just those where psychological satisfaction is likely to be obtained. Herzberg's (1959) popular theory of motivation explicitly stated this and a similar conclusion could be drawn from Maslow's (1943) influential motivation model. Yet the ideological implications of such contentions are evident enough and they offer, just as Shell's new philosophy came to do, an apparent rationale for the essential acceptability of the 'status quo'. Unfortunately, though, it is self evident that a person's job satisfaction, by his own standards, may not necessarily have much to do with his satis-factoriness in that job, judged by someone elses.

There are a number of possible responses to an aware-ness of such points. One response would be to ignore their significance. To the extent socio-technical theorists have, as we suggested, ignored comments concerning the limitations of their craft this response can, perhaps, be identified. An alternative reaction would be to concentrate on the significance of O.D. or socio-technical theory for productivity, rather than for satisfaction. The considerable growth in 'contingency' models for this or that illustrates this response (see for example Lawrence and Lorsch's 1967 contingency O.D. model or Lupton's 1975 contingency approach to job design). A further reaction to the discovery that conditions favouring worker fulfilment may not be those associated with their productivity would be to withdraw from conventional applied social science endeavours lest they involve compromise or unintended manipulation. This may be a more common reaction than is generally realised; perhaps Max Pages (1974) expression of sentiments along just these lines

163

reflects other peoples reactions to the lost promises
of the T-group movement of the 1960's as well. Lastly,
a possible reaction to a discovery of the pitfalls of
attempts to apply, in the stark reality of the
industrial world, certain social science ideas born of
idealism would be to reformulate the theoretical framework one was working with. This is, perhaps less in
evidence as a response than might be hoped. Yet some
notable developments have occurred. Relevant to our
discussion is Gustavsen's (1977) report about how
socio-technical work in Norway has been widened to
include legislation provisions supporting and
broadening attempts to introduce democracy at shop
floor level. Regarding O.D., advances have been made
here with, for example, Pettigrew's (1975) work marking
a response to appeals for O.D. people to recognise more
the realities of organisational power, and with
Mangham's (1978) usage of the dramaturgical analogy for
understanding the dynamics of change representing a
much needed departure from the hybrid blend of systems
theory and humanistic psychology that hitherto has
dominated thinking in this area.

Just as the pseudo-innocence of the Shell story has
a relevance for today so, too, do the lessons that may
be learned from an application of the fluoridation
model for change. That the same basic confidence in
the package presented to Shell is still held today by
some of those originally involved is not hard to see.
Interviewed for the magazine 'International Management'
(June 1978 edition) Fred Emery described a format for
holding managerial conferences (he calls them 'search'
conferences) in organisations. At such meetings Emery
invites managers to reflect on the various factors
affecting their efforts and to consider possible and
desirable ways of responding to them. While such a
strategy seems sensible and neutral enough it is
interesting to note that in this same article Emery
refers to the programme of philosophy conferences in
Shell in the 1960's as evidence of just what can be
done at such meetings. This would suggest that Emery
is still, at his 'search' conferences, presenting the
same kind of global analysis and package of solutions

that he and his co-workers first tried at Shell over a
decade before.

Within O.D. too there is much evidence that 'package'
solutions are presented to managers under the guise of
a methodology to help them solve their own problems.
In his typology of approaches to O.D. for example Blake
(1976) suggests that the most advanced forms of interventions in organisation are those based on 'principles'
providing a yardstick against which present behaviours
may be judged. Nor surprisingly Blake's own 'Grid'
method of training is cited as an example of such an
intervention strategy. Yet such package approaches can
be criticised on theoretical grounds (Argyris's famous
1970 presentation of a theory of effective intervention,
for example very clearly stated the pitfalls of such
methods) and on empirical ones also. Lourenco (1976),
for example, analysed the outcomes of a consultant's
intervention using a package approach and discussed how
it led to disappointments and to latent conflicts. The
most dramatic illustration of the blindness of such
approaches that we are aware of, however, was reported
by Berlew and LeClere (1974) and involved the introduction of motivation and group dynamics training to
the population of Curacao, a small island in the
Caribbean. Despite tremendous enthusiasm and initial
efforts this project failed to have the decisive impact
on the culture of the island that had been sought by
the American consultants involved. In a commentary on
the failure of this case Korten (1974) posed the
question of how it was that the change agents under-
estimated the formidable difficulties in the way of
their self devised objective to set goals for a small
nation. He wrote:

> 'Why did the consultants misread the signals
> and broaden the goals of the project? Part of
> the answer to this lies, I think, outside of
> the case as it is presented. I recall quite
> clearly the early enthusiasm of a number of
> close friends who were involved in the Curacao
> intervention. The excitement and commitment
> were genuine, spontaneous, and very contagious.

165

Here was a project not only with objectives in which they fully believed but one which was also a great deal of fun. I was frankly jealous of them at the time and would have jumped at a chance to participate. Here was an opportunity for which many members of our profession must secretly dream - an opportunity to reshape, or so it seemed, an entire society of a size sufficiently small that a small group of con- sultants might have a major impact. The Islands' recent crisis seemed to have created an openness to change and new solutions, a ready made laboratory. What an attraction!'

The excitement that Korten refers to here sounds indeed, not unlike that we have suggested was characteristic of the Shell programme and clearly there is something of a general problem here for applied social science. To become significantly involved in an action programme requires that anyone, social scientist or layman, be committed to the work he or she is under- taking. A degree of confidence, faith, hope or just tough mindedness is a necessary part of the involvement. Yet to the extent he or she is more scientist than salesman the applied scientist needs to experience doubts and to recognise the possibility that even a basic revision of his position could be required. Herein lies a dilemma: to embark on new ventures requires a certain confidence, to accept the discipline of a scientific approach necessitates a certain caution and reflectiveness.

There are two major consequences of any failure to ride this dilemma satisfactorily. The first we have seen in the Shell case where, as we have previously noted, the good intentions of the social scientists involved were not enough. The inadequacies of the analysis they were working with, coupled with their mode of presentation, created in the project certain manipulative undercurrents. In his book 'Alternatives to Hierarchies' the socio-technical theorist Phil Herbst notes the possibility of social science being used to create new techniques of social control. Yet

the comments he makes in the same book on the Shell
case itself suggests he is quite unaware that the Shell
story provides evidence of just such an occurence. It
is our view that if overconfidence and naivety remain
hallmarks of the applied social scientist then much
more will need to be written in years to come on how
bureaucratic methods of organisational control have
become substituted by 'sociocratic' ones.

   The second major consequence of a failure to combine
commitment with reflection concerns the prospects for
the development of applied social science as a science.
At the start of this chapter we observed how social
psychologists have long desired their work to be
relevant to social problems and how the package of
ideas associated with the analysis of turbulent
environments and socio-technical systems offers great
promise in this respect. Our point here was that it is
tempting to dismiss possible criticisms of such
approaches as being unnecessarily destructive. In his
discussion of the problems of any newly emerging and
immature science Ravetz (1971) makes the point that
special care in respect of such temptations is
necessary. While Ravetz couches his discussion in
general terms and refers to no particular example of
an immature science the points he makes fit the
situation in applied social psychology exactly.
Consider the following analysis he offers of possible
developments within a newly emerging theoretical area:

   'In the modern situation, we have many examples
   of successful special "arts" arising out of
   inquiries in immature or even nascent fields.
   These will usually be methods for solving
   technical problems which, although very
   restricted in comparison with the goals of the
   field as a whole are quite useful. It is known
   from experience that the methods work, and a
   body of genuine craft skills can be developed
   for the tasks; even though the theory on which
   the method was first based may have been dis-
   credited, and no scientifically satisfactory
   explanation has been produced. It is a natural

167

error to cite such arts as evidence for the maturity of the field, as if they arose as applications of a solidly established body of fact'. (Ravetz, 1971, p.373)

It is our view that this paragraph could have been written with the Shell project in mind. Certainly also anyone familiar with the literature on organisational development could be forgiven for thinking that Ravetz was describing the state of affairs within O.D. Indeed, the summary of Kahn's (1974) review of O.D. begins:

'Examination of the rapidly increasing body of O.D. literature reveals that much of its research is redundant and without refinement or validation, that the term "Organisational Development" itself remains scientifically undefined and hence primarily a convenient label for a variety of activities, and that the O.D. literature as a whole is more autobiographical than organisational in focus and scope'. (Kahn, 1974, p.485)

Kahn's review served to remind O.D. practitioners that, despite the hopes and the voluminous literature associated with their work, it is far from being based on 'scientific' principles. Such a reminder is well issued to applied social scientists for, as Ravetz continues in his general analysis of the pitfalls in immature sciences, if the limited nature of work in such a field is not recognised and a 'small core of successful craft techniques and aphoristic wisdom is embedded in a doctrine imitating a mature science' serious problems will arise. 'Cliché-science' is the term he uses to describe the outcomes of such a process. This state would be achieved when the original and genuine insights that first emerged in the immature science are later overplayed. What would appear in these circumstances is a product containing the trappings, but not the substance, of a mature area of science.

As a final comment we would emphasise that it has not been our intention to be unnecessarily carping in

making these points. Regarding the case around which
this book is written we are aware that the full extent
of the disappointments associated with it were not
previously known and whatever use one might now want
to say about it the philosophy exercise was surely a
brave attempt in what it tried to do. But while there
are lessons to be learned by treating the Shell story
as a 'gallant failure' this on its own is not enough.
Nor, in the light of Ravetz's warning about the
problems of immature disciplines, and the potential
for clichés to emerge within them in place of insights
would it be in the best interests of science. To the
extent that applied social scientists are concerned
both with the development of genuinely social
applications of their ideas and with a vigorous development of the ideas themselves the Shell story must
stand as something of a cautionary tale.

Appendix

SHELL REFINING COMPANY LIMITED

DRAFT STATEMENT OF OBJECTIVES AND PHILOSOPHY (May 1966)

I Primary objective

Shell Refining Company is primarily concerned to maximise its contribution to the long-term profitability of the Shell Group insofar as this arises from the efficiency with which it uses the Group's resources of men, money and material.

The resources to which it has legal rights of privileged access are nonetheless part of the total resources of society as a whole and are, in this sense, social resources; the Company believes that they must be protected, developed and managed as such. It furthermore believes that its use of these resources must be such as to contribute to meeting society's requirements for products and services.

The Company recognises, however, that ultimate discretion for what can be done to maximise Group profitability cannot properly be exercised without having a total picture of the exploration, production, transportation, manufacturing, marketing and research functions. Since the activities of Shell Refining Company lie mainly within the manufacturing function, this makes necessary the statement of its specific objectives in terms of the minimum expenditure of resources appropriate to the discharge of its responsibilities to the Group.

II Specific objectives

Specifically this commits the Company to:-

(a) meeting the current market requirements
for refined petroleum products with minimum
expenditure of total resources per unit of
quantity of given quality, and

(b) ensuring the Company's ability to meet
emerging market requirements with decreasing
expenditure of total resources per unit of
of quantity of specified quality.

An essential task of Management is to seek at all
times optimal solutions to (a) and (b).

In addition, the Company is specifically committed by
its position in the Group to:-

(c) seeking continually from the Group the
power and the information necessary to enable
it to meet its responsibilities.

In certain circumstances it may be necessary
to seek a re-definition of its responsibilities
in order that the Company's capabilities may
be best used on behalf of the Group.

Implicit in these three specific objectives and in
the fact that the Company's resources are part of the
total resources of society, are the following additional specific objectives:-

(d) creating conditions in which employees at
all levels will be encouraged and enabled to
develop and to realise their potentialities
while contributing towards the Company's
objectives;

(e) carrying out its productive and other
operations in such a way as to safeguard the
health and safety of its employees and the
public;

(f) seeking to reduce any interference that
may be caused by its activities to the amenities

of the community, accepting the measures
practised under comparable conditions in
British industry as a minimum standard and
making use of the expertise and knowledge
available within the Group.

III The principle of joint-optimisation as a guide to
implementation

The Company must manage both a social system, of people
and their organisation, and a technical system, of
physical equipment and resources. Optimisation of its
overall operations can be achieved only by jointly
optimising the operation of these two systems; attempts
to optimise the two independently of each other, or
undue emphasis upon one of them at the expense or the
neglect of the other, must fail to achieve optimisation
for the Company as a whole.

IV Key characteristics of the evolving technical
system

In order to create appropriate conditions for the
optimisation of the overall system, it is necessary to
design the social system jointly with the technical
system recognising that the latter has certain key
persistent characteristics which must be taken into
account. These characteristics are:-

(a) The Company forms part of a complex,
science-based industry subject to rapid
technical change. This rate of change can be
expected to increase in the future.

(b) There is a wide measure of flexibility
available in all the main processes involved
in oil refining, i.e. distillation, conversion
and blending. The added value which results
from refining operations depends to a high
degree upon the skilful use of this flexibility
in plant design and operation and the programming
of refinery and overall Company operations in
order to meet variable market requirements from

given and variable inputs.

(c)   The Company is capital-intensive and it
follows that adequate criteria of overall
Company performance must be sought mainly in
measures of efficiency of plant utilisation.
The importance to overall Company performance
of efficient plant utilisation makes necessary
a high degree of plant reliability.

(d)   The Company's refineries are already
highly involved with automation and instrumentation. Pressure for a very much higher level of
automation and instrumentation arises from the
development of new processes and the drive
towards optimal use of the flexibility described
in (b) above, and the need to improve the
ability to control, identify and account for
the large number of movements through the
technical system at any one time.

(e)   There is considerable variation in the
degree of automation of different operations in
the Company. Labour-intensive activities exist
side by side with highly automated ones. Despite
the trends noted in (a) and (b) above, some
variation is likely to persist.

(f)   The Company's process operations are
carried out on a continuous 24 hours per day,
seven day week basis, by a number of shift teams,
while many associated service activities are
carried out discontinuously on a day working
basis.

(g)   The refineries and Head Office are
geographically widely separated and within
refineries there is a considerable dispersion
of the various activities. For economic and
technical reasons this characteristic is
likely to persist.

V Implications for the social system

The rapid and increasing rate of change in the technical system defined in characteristic (a) creates a special need for new expertise, skills and knowledge at all levels, and new forms of organisation to cope with changing requirements. It also increases the rate at which skills and knowledge are rendered obsolete. The Company believes that its objectives in relation to the social nature of its resources commit it to train its employees in new skills and new knowledge where obsolesence of skills and knowledge has resulted from its own or the industry's technical development. These effects require the Company to plan for the development of appropriate skills and forms of organisation in parallel with the planning of technical change.

The most significant consequence of characteristics (b), (c), (d), (f) and (g) is that economic production within our process technology is critically dependent upon people effectively dealing with information yielded by the technical system and contributing the most appropriate information to the control and guidance of that system. Some of these informational flows are confined to individuals who take information from the technical system and feed back guidance directly into it. Other informational flows must be carried at any one time by a network of many people at many different organisational levels. The effectiveness of this social informational network depends upon the recognition by all those involved in its design and operation that it is made up of people and is therefore affected by the factors that influence human behaviour.

The wide geographical dispersion of the refineries and the extensive layout within the refineries themselves present an impediment to effective communications. This makes it even more necessary for the Company to design efficient informational flows.

A further consequence of characteristic (c), namely the need for a high degree of plant reliability is that economic production is also highly dependent upon the application of craft skills and knowledge.

In information handling and to a large degree in the
exercise of craft skills, the problem is to avoid
lapses of attention and errors in observing, diagnosing
and communicating or acting upon information. Information handling work in the refining industry is such
that lapses and errors are likely to result in heavy
costs, both from delay in recognising errors and taking
corrective action and from the nature of the equipment
and the processes involved. The only promising way of
avoiding these faults is for the individual to be
internally motivated to exercise responsibility and
initiative. Any external control can only act after
the error has occurred or had its effect.

In contrast, in those jobs where the main human
contribution is manual labour, there is some choice as
to how control may be achieved. Although optimal
control requires internal motivation, the shortcomings
associated with mainly manual tasks do not normally
result in heavy costs and it is possible to achieve an
economic degree of control by external incentives and
supervision. For these reasons the exercise of
personal responsibility and initiative in such work,
although desirable, may be considered less significant.

However, the manual jobs in the refineries
(characteristic (e)) exist mainly amongst service
activities ancillary to the operating and engineering
activities which are central to the task of oil
refining. It is considered essential that the Company's
philosophy should be appropriate to the nature of these
central activities. For those activities of a
different nature it may be necessary to modify them
through technical developments, e.g. the introduction
of mechanisation or automation, or to develop other
social systems appropriate to them, in keeping with the
values of the Company's philosophy.

Despite the complication arising from characteristic
(e) therefore, the major implication of this group of
technical characteristics emerges as the need to

develop a high level of personal responsibility and initiative.

VI Responsibility and commitment

People cannot be expected to develop within themselves and to exercise the level of responsibility and initiative that is required unless they can be involved in their task and unless, in the long run, it is possible to develop commitment to the objectives served by their task.

The Company recognises that it cannot expect its employees at all levels to develop adequate involvement and commitment spontaneously or in response to mere exhortation. It must set out to create the conditions under which such commitment may develop.

The work of social scientists has shown that the creation of such conditions cannot be achieved simply by the provision of satisfactory terms of service, including renumeration. The provision of such terms of service is essential, but is not in itself sufficient; for involvement and commitment at all levels it is necessary to go beyond this, to meet the general psychological requirements that men have of their work.

The following are some of the psychological requirements that relate to the content of a job:-

    (a) The need for the content of the work to be reasonably demanding of the individual in terms other than those of sheer endurance, and for it to provide some variety.

    (b) The need for an individual to know what his job is and how he is performing in it.

    (c) The need to be able to learn on the job and go on learning.

    (d) The need for some area of decision making where the individual can exercise his discretion.

(e) The need for some degree of social support and recognition within the organisation.

(f) The need for an individual to be able to relate what he does and what he produces to the objectives of the Company and to his life in the community.

(g) The need to feel that the job leads to some sort of desirable future which does not necessarily imply promotion.

These requirements exist in some form for the large majority of men and at all levels of employment. Their relative significance, however, will clearly vary from individual to individual and it is not possible to provide for their fulfilment in the same way for all kinds of people. Similarly, different jobs will provide varying degrees of opportunity for the fulfilment of particular requirements.

They cannot generally be met, however, simply by re-designing individual jobs. Most tasks involve more than one person and, in any case, all jobs must be organisationally related to the Company's objectives. If the efforts to meet the above requirements for individuals are not to be frustrated, the Company must observe certain principles in developing its organisational form. Thus, the individual must know not only what he is required to do, but also the way in which his work ties in with what others are doing, the part he plays in the communications network, and the limits within which he has genuine discretionary powers. Furthermore, the individual's responsibilities should be defined in terms of objectives to be pursued; although procedural rules are necessary for co-ordination, they must be reviewed regularly in the light of experience gained in pursuing these objectives.

Responsibility and authority must go hand in hand in order to avoid situations in which people are delegated responsibility but do not have the means to exercise it. Likewise, the Company must be ready to redefine responsibilities where there are capabilities which are unused.

Not least, the Company must seek to ensure that the distribution of status and reward is consistent with the level of responsibility carried by the individual.

In following this course the Company will seek the fullest involvement of all employees and will make the best use of available knowledge and experience of the social sciences.

VII   Principle of implementation of the philosophy

The effective implementation and communication of the philosophy throughout the Company can be achieved only if its mode of implementation manifests the spirit of the philosophy. Verbal or written communication alone will not suffice; it is essential that all employees be enabled to relate the philosophy to themselves by participating in the implementation of the philosophy in their particular parts of the Company.

A special burden of responsibility must rest with the senior managers, who alone are in a position to exercise the leadership and provide the necessary impetus to translate the philosophy into a living reality. Starting with their commitment, it will be possible to involve progressively the other levels of the employees in searching out the implications for themselves. As the philosophy begins to shape the activities of the Company it will be able more effectively to pursue its objectives.

Bibliography

Anderson, G., 'The South Australian Initiative', in Pritchard, R. (ed), Industrial Democracy in Australia, CCH Press, 1976.

Alderfer, C.P., 'Organisation Development', Annual Review of Psychology, 28, 1977, pp.197-223.

Argyris, C., Intervention Theory and Method, Addison Wesley, Reading, Mass. 1970.

Armistead, N., Reconstructing Social Psychology, Penguin, Harmondsworth 1974.

Baritz, L., The Servants of Power, Wesleyan Connecticut University Press, 1960.

Bell, D., The End of Ideology, Collier Books, New York 1961.

Berlew, D.E. and LeClere, W.E., 'Social Intervention in Curacao: A Case Study', Journal of Applied Behavioural Science, 10, 1974, pp.29-52.

Blackler, F.H.M. and Brown, C.A., Job Redesign and Management Control, Saxon House, London 1978.

Blake, R.R. and Mouton, J.S., Consultation, Addison Wesley, Reading 1976.

Bolweg, J.F., Job Design and Industrial Democracy, Martinus Nijhoff, Leiden 1976.

Braverman, H., Labor and Monopoly Capital, Monthly Review Press, New York 1974.

Bucklow, M., 'A New Role for the Work Group', Administrative Science Quarterly, no.11, 1966, pp.59-78.

Burden, D.W.E., 'Participative management as a basis
for improved quality of jobs: the case of the micro-
wax department Shell UK Ltd.', in Davis, L.E. and
Cherns, A.B. (eds), The Quality of Working Life
Volume II, Collier-McMillan, New York 1975.

Clark, A., 'Sanction, A Critical Element in Action
Research', Journal of Applied Behavioural Science,
8, 1972, pp.713-31.

Emery, F.E. and Emery, M., A Choice of Futures,
Martinus Nijhoff, Leiden 1976.

Emery, F.E. and Oeser, O.A., Information, Decision and
Action, Melbourne University Press, 1958.

Emery, F.E. and Thorsrud, E., Form and Content in
Industrial Democracy, Tavistock, London 1969.

Emery, F.E. and Trist, E.L., 'The Causal Texture of
Organisational Environments', Human Relations, 18,
1965, pp.21-32.

Emery, F.E. and Trist, E.L., Towards a Social Ecology:
Contextual Appreciation of the Future in the Present,
Plenum, London 1972.

Flanders, A., The Fawley Productivity Agreements,
Faber and Faber, London 1964.

Foster, M., 'An Introduction to the Theory and Practice
of Action Research in Work Organisations', Human
Relations, 25, 1972, pp.529-56.

Fox, A., 'The Meaning of Work', in People and Work,
Block 3, Unit 6, Open University Press, Milton Keynes
1976.

French, W.L. and Bell, C.H., Organisation Development,
Prentice Hall, New Jersey 1973.

Friedmann, G., Industrial Society, Free Press, New
York 1955.

Gulowsen, J., 'A Measure of Work-Group Autonomy', in
   Davis, L.E. and Taylor, J.C. (eds), <u>Design of Jobs</u>,
   Penguin, London 1972.

Gustavsen, B., 'A Legislative Approach to Job Reform in
   Norway, <u>International Labour Review</u>, 115, 1977,
   pp.263-76.

Gyllenhammar, P., <u>People at Work</u>, Addison Wesley,
   Reading 1977.

Herbst, P.G., <u>Sociotechnical Design: Strategies in
   Multidisciplinary Research</u>, Tavistock, London 1974.

Herbst, P.G., <u>Alternatives to Hierarchies</u>, Martinus
   Nijhoff, The Hague 1976.

Herzberg, F., Mausner, B. and Snyderman, B.B., <u>The
   Motivation to Work</u>, Wiley, New York 1959.

Hibbert, G.G., <u>Identification of a need for Social
   Science Input and Some Applications in a Major Oil
   Refining Company</u>, unpublished M.Sc., Loughborough
   University 1969.

Hill, P., <u>Towards a New Philosophy of Management</u>,
   Gower Press, London 1971.

Kahn, R.L., 'Organisational Development: Some Problems
   and Proposals', <u>Journal of Applied Behavioural
   Science</u>, 10, 1974, pp.485-502.

Korten, D.C., 'Comments on "Social Intervention in
   Curacao" by Berlew and LeClere', <u>Journal of Applied
   Behavioural Science</u>, 10, 1974, pp.53-60.

Kumar, K., <u>Prophecy and Progress</u>, Penguin, Harmondsworth 1978.

Lawrence, P.R. and Lorsch, J.W., <u>Organisation and
   Environment</u>, Irwin, Homewood, Illinois 1967.

Likert, R., New Patterns of Management, McGraw Hill, London 1961.

Lourenco, S.V., 'Conflict and Failure in Planned Change', Human Relations, 29, 1976, pp.1189-1203.

Lupton, T., 'Efficiency and the Quality of Worklife: The Technology of Reconciliation', Organisational Dynamics, 4, 1975, pp.68-80.

McGregor, D., The Human Side of Enterprise, McGraw Hill, London 1961.

Mangham, I.L., Interactions and Interventions in Organisations, Wiley, Chichester 1978.

Marrow, A.J., The Practical Theorist: The Life and Work of Kurt Lewin, Basic Books, New York 1969.

May, R., Power and Innocence, Norton, New York 1972.

Nichols, T., 'Management Ideology and Practice', in People at Work, Block 4, Unit 15, Open University Press, Milton Keynes 1976.

Nord, W., 'The Failure of Current Applied Behavioural Science: A Marxian Perspective', Journal of Applied Behavioural Science, 10, 1974, pp.557-78.

Pages, M., 'An Interview with Max Pages', Journal of Applied Behavioural Science, 10, 1974, pp.8-26.

Pettigrew, A.M., 'Towards a Political Theory of Organisational Intervention', Human Relations, 28, 1976, pp.191-208.

Qvale, T.U., 'A Norwegian Strategy for Democratization of Industry', Human Relations, 29, 1976, pp.453-69.

Rein, M.R., Social Science and Public Policy, Penguin, Harmondsworth 1976.

Rosow, J.M. (ed), The Worker and the Job, Prentice

Hall, London 1974.

Roszak, T., The Making of a Counter Culture, Faber and Faber, London 1970.

Sanford, N., 'Whatever Happened to Action Research?', Journal of Social Issues, 26, 1970.

Stevenson, T.E., 'Organisation Development: A Critique', Journal of Management Studies, 12, 1975, pp.249-65.

Tannenbaum, R. and Davis, S., 'Values, Man and Organisations', Industrial Management Review, 10, 1969, pp.68-70.

Taylor, L.K., Not for Bread Alone: An Appreciation of Job Enrichment, Business Books Ltd., London 1972(a).

Taylor, L.K., 'Job Enrichment at Shell Stanlow', Hydrocarbon Processing, June 1972(b), pp.140-4.

Thorsrud, E. and Emery, F., Democracy at Work: A Report of the Norwegian Industrial Democracy Programme, Martinus Nijhoff, Leiden 1976.

Tizard, J., 'Psychology and Social Policy', Bulletin of the British Psychological Society, 29, 1976, pp.225-34.

Trist, E.L., 'Technical, Social and Cultural Developments and their Implications for People in Organisations', paper presented at the 1st European Forum on Organisation Development, Aachen 1978. To be reproduced in Trebesch, K. (ed), Organisation Development in Europe, P.H. Verlag, Berne 1980.

Trist, E.L., Higgin, G.W., Murray, H. and Pollock, A.B., Organisational Choice, Tavistock, London 1963.

Walton, R.E., 'The Diffusion of New Work Structures: Explaining Why Success Didn't Take', Organisational Dynamics, Winter 1975, p.3-22.

Woodward, J., _Industrial Organisation: Theory and Practice_, Oxford University Press, 1965.